THIS IS A DO-IT-YOURSELF, SELF-HELP, HOW-TO, PREVENTIVE HEALTH BOOK PACKED WITH SENSIBLE, POSITIVE, AND HEALTHY ADVICE ABOUT:

THIN *VS.* FAT
Growing up Nourished-Yet-Thin
Fat Runs in Families
The Fat Psychology
Anxiety and Fatness

LIVING TO EAT OR EATING TO LIVE
Good Nutrition and Disease Resistance
Fibers, Fruits, and Fighting Illness
Cholesterol and Heart Disease

BRAINS, SUGAR, AND THE NAKED CALORIE
Nutrition and I.Q.
Liberation from Sugar
The Hidden Calories in a Sugar-Coated Culture

FROM SOUPS TO NUTS
How to Sneak Vegetables by Your Kids
Meatless Meals
Egging a Child On
Secret Sources of Protein
The Whole Grain Catalog

How to convert the kids from what they eat to what they oughta

by Polly Greenberg

BALLANTINE BOOKS · NEW YORK

To my beautiful eighteen year old daughter Katie, because it's the year of the Kate, and also because she's making such an admirable, valiant effort to consume less Coke and cookies, and more fruits and vegetables.

With gratitude to my daughter Julie's high school biology teacher, Mr. Podgorney, whose first name and whereabouts I do not know, and whom I have never met; but who helped *her* to eat more wisely. She, in turn, helped *me* to cook more wisely. This helped all the other children in our family to eat more wisely *out* of the house as well as in it and this has helped some of their friends, and so it goes on.

Here's hoping this brief "applied nutrition" book will help others who've been wanting to move in these healthier directions for a while, but have been lacking aid in organizing and focusing their effort. Julie, my love, thank *you* for organizing and focusing *me*.

Library of Congress Catalog Card Number: 79-57070

ISBN 0-345-28784-3

This edition published by arrangement with Kaplan Press

Manufactured in the United States of America

First Ballantine Books Edition: April 1980

Introduction

This is a do-it-yourself, self-help, how-to, preventive health book. It provides a step-by-step ten month way to convert from what you eat to what you "oughta." It provides a process for helping children become involved in taking responsibility for feeding themselves more healthily. The first section talks about *why* many health specialists think Americans should change their basic eating habits. The second section suggests *how* to do so, and includes hundreds of food ideas.

This is neither a "nut" book, nor a book passionately advocating that people entirely eliminate sugar from their diet, eat fiber twelve times a day, and at all costs avoid falling victim to an egg or a potato chip. It is *not* pushing one frontier of nutritional research or theory or another, or any specific and lopsided fad promoted by one or another group of nutritionists or concerned consumers. Rather it can help adults come to realize that they have the personal power to alter the most serious defects in their own and children's regular eating patterns—*defects as defined almost universally by nutrition authorities.*

Parents and teachers aren't "to blame" if all doesn't go well in the lives of the children in their care, because other factors and fates beyond the control of these caretaking adults may affect children. Yet parents and teachers *do* have a lot of power to determine the directions in which childrens' habits, interests, preferences, behavior, and attitudes will go. The younger the child, the more this is true. Preschool children are homebound. They experience very, very little that their parents, guardians, or substitute childcarers hired by parents or guardians don't make possible by providing or by passively "allowing." If we wish, we parents *are* capable of being nutrition conversion "project managers" for the family.

Once children start early childhood education programs or school, more nonhome influences can reach them. Teachers' influence is enormous. Teachers at all grade levels will find ideas here that they can use in their classrooms and as homework projects. This conversion plan is ten months long. Ten months is a school year.

Even after children start school, parents structure what happens at home. We strongly influence what our children think and do *outside* our homes, too. Children 8-12 years of age may be heavily influenced by peers, but parents and teachers still have the means and the responsibility to guide children in all important areas. As long as we continue to act as if American children are well-nourished, instead of noticing the incredible amount of sugar, salt, chemicals, and other undesirables they consume, we can't give the firm guidance we otherwise could.

Even teenagers know and care what the adults they respect think, particularly if relations have been solid and happy before the teen years begin. Some teenagers have self-destructive tendencies, and indulge to a dangerous degree in drugs, drink, or dangerous driving. Probably many more *like* themselves sufficiently well to take care of themselves, and *would* eat less horrendously, if we tempted them to help themselves to better health "by mouth."

Parents and teachers can guide children toward fairly healthy basic eating patterns, or can fail to do so. Whether adults decide to take an active role in shaping children's eating patterns depends upon many things. One of these is how important parents and teachers think health *is*.

Many Americans feel so healthy so much of the time that they don't think much about it, or do much about it. They just *assume* health. They assume that their children will, fundamentally, be healthy. Other people focus on illness. When we or the children are ill or injured, we call upon the doctor's services.

Doctors are not preventive health specialists. They're trained to catch and, if possible, cure, things that are going wrong. Cancer and heart specialists can't develop well people and keep them healthy. This isn't their major interest and they aren't *there,* in residence, in homes and classrooms, to give developmental health guidance. Few homes or classrooms have a family physician or pediatrician in daily residence to be responsible for the development of a life-style of healthy habits: a pattern of sleeping right, exercising right, and eating right—*all* of which give people better resistance to germs and viruses.

Because there are no other constantly available preventive health specialists, those parents, teachers, and others in charge of children who highly value health *must take the responsibility to oversee the gradual growth of healthy behaviors and attitudes.* Scientists, physicians, nutritionists and related experts can shed information to the right and to the left, but until parents and teachers *apply* it, it's only fun and games for the experts, and it won't help us.

Another factor that determines the degree to which adults will attempt to influence the eating patterns of the children in their care is whether or not these adults believe that the children's eating patterns are unwise. Intensely grim nutritionists and intensely grim health food faddists can twist our arms all they like, but unless we grownups who raise and educate the children apply the advice given to us, the children's eating patterns will remain unaffected. Nutritionists do not stock our houses with groceries, prepare food for the family, and let children know what they're allowed to eat when they're out. *We* do.

Further factors influencing whether or not adults take a positive and active role in developing children's eating habits are:

- Whether or not they *know* what nutrition specialists recommend;
- Whether or not they see how all the welter of advice fits together, so they know what they should do;
- Whether or not they understand the methods and techniques of *applying* all this to the lives of the children they love.

The author of this book is not a nutritionist and has no new nutrition information to offer. She *is* a child development person whose specialty is helping parents and teachers *apply* what research and specialty professions know if these parents and teachers want such help. She is also the working mother of five, who isn't much interested in cooking, but who loves happy meals with her children, and who cares that they develop life-protecting, sensible dietry patterns. The unique aspect here is the focus on making it easier and interesting for ordinary people who are not particularly interested in shopping, cooking, and nutrition to apply some of the information which nutritionists and health educators have been disseminating (relatively unsuccessfully) for generations. The book will be of no use to those who are already experts on eating healthily, or to those who don't think healthy eating is important.

The purposes of HOW TO CONVERT THE KIDS FROM WHAT THEY EAT TO WHAT THEY OUGHTA are:

- to *interest* parents and teachers in *examining the eating patterns of the children for whom they are responsible* (adults frequently don't even realize how terrible these eating patterns are);
- to contrast these patterns for each child in their adult care with major dangers and problems in American eating habits *upon which most nutrition experts agree* (and only the ones on which most agree);
- to help adults see practical, *non-overwhelming,* one-at-a-time steps they can take to begin "food safing" the home and the classroom;

- to begin significantly improving their own *eating* patterns; and
- to begin a *gradual, ten-month project of motivating each child to track his own eating habits,* gain knowledge about wise eating, *and take on the responsibility for managing his own nutritional life* for long-term better health.

Though all human personalities grow according to certain developmental principles and share certain characteristics, each individual personality is different. Similarly, all human bodies grow according to developmental principles and share some characteristics; but in some respects, each individual's biology is different. Because of individual genetics, allergies, illnesses, and other conditions, general recommendations offered in the following chapters may be superceded by doctors' orders. This book is for nonexceptional people. The contents of this guide to better nutrition are common sensible.

Hypertension, heart disease, cancer, and life-spoiling emotional problems have reached epidemic proportions in this country. Medical authorities think all of them are diet-related. Though eternal life and perfect health are not options available to us, and though there's no way to get a guarantee against illness, better health through better nutrition is an option we can pursue if we think it important. We all believe in health. We *don't* all help it happen.

Food is an emotion-filled, as well as a calorie-filled, subject. Advice cannot be given on this topic without eliciting a barrage of counteradvice, heated attacks, and skeptically raised eyebrows. However, here we go, in hopes that at least a few people will find what follows helpful in developing life-long eating patterns and greater resistance to a wide variety of physical, mental, emotional and social ills.

Table of Contents

Table of Contents

Table of Contents

PART ONE:

How and Why
to Convert

CHAPTER ONE:

How to Start the Conversion

First, Individual Assessment: Recording "Reality"

To begin converting, the homemaker and everybody else from about nine to ninety who is taking part in the process keeps *honest* written records of all foods eaten during a one-week period. No effort should be made to do anything more. The homemaker records *all* foods he or she serves at all meals and snacks, including ingredients. The homemaker also records what each individual under nine years of age eats between meals. Everything that goes into the mouth counts, including gum, cough drops, vitamin pills, and everything else.

This is an excellent activity for kindergarten, primary, elementary, high school, and college teachers to carry out as part of health education, or science. Teachers can suggest the conversion project to parents. Parents can suggest it to teachers. Most people enjoy doing it because they learn a lot about themselves, and most of them are fascinated by what they learn.

Second, Classifying Results: What Kind of Food Was It?

Next, we examine our eating-habit notes, keeping in mind these classifications:

THE "EAT-MORE" FOODS

- Fruit and fruit juices (not fruit *drinks* or fruit flavored "fake" drinks such as Kool-Aid—only fresh, frozen, or canned "straight" juices)

- Vegetables (may be fresh, frozen, or canned)
- Fish and poultry
- Cheese (*not* processed cheese and cheese spreads; must be *real* cheese; cottage cheese is best of all)
- Legumes, nuts and seeds (legumes are lentils, split peas, black eye peas, chick peas, kidney beans, lima beans, soy beans, etc.)
- Grain foods: breads, crackers, pies, cakes, cookies, candies made with rye or whole wheat grain (*not* instant or white rice); whole grain cereals (without sugar coatings); and whole grain pastas (*not* white pastas)
- Skim milk and milk products

THE "EAT-MUCH-LESS" FOODS

- Meat (lean beef, veal, lamb, and pork, and remember that pork products have excessive calories and cholesterol in comparison to the nutrients they provide)
- Chemicals (food coloring and food flavoring especially; preservatives where possible; and other chemicals)
- Sugar (includes baked goodies, syrups, jams, white and brown sugar, and sugar listed as a first, second or third ingredient in something) and honey
- Calories in excess of those in an equivalent food, nutritionally speaking. For example, among meats, veal, beef, and lamb have far fewer calories than pork.
- Cholesterol (avoid eggs more than four times a week, fatty meats altogether, and meat more than four times a week; avoid cheese on meat eating days so as not to get too much cholesterol all at once)
- Salt (avoid cooking and baking with salt, salting food at the table, and buying heavily salted snack foods such as potato chips, pretzels, seeds and nuts —buy the *un*salted seeds and nuts)
- Coffee, tea and alcohol (no more than two cups a day of coffee or tea; nor more than a drink or two a day)

Third, Comparing All That A Person Ate With Amounts Recommended

Thirdly, we compare the record of what we and each child ate during the week to rough recommendations for the general population (except for people who've personally been told by a doctor to follow other guidelines for reasons related to their own individual physiology.) The generally recommended foods are:

- Two to four fruits or fruit juices daily, one a citrus fruit, if possible (large or smaller portion according to the age of the person).
- One green and one yellow vegetable—raw or cooked, fresh, frozen, or canned—daily, plus as many more as the person wants (except corn, which contains fewer of the nutrients than expected in a yellow vegetable and too much sugar).
- A serving of meat (beef, veal, or lamb) no more than three or four times a week (including breakfast meats, sandwich meats, and dinner meats) or meat as an *ingredient* in a dish no more than seven times a week. (It is *not* necessary to eat meat at all; vegetarians should daily eat legumes, nuts, seeds, fish, cheese or eggs to obtain needed protein).
- Fish and poultry twice a week, or as often as desired.
- No more than three or four eggs a week (this includes breakfast eggs, egg salad, egg dinner dishes), plus the amount of egg eaten as an ingredient in something else like cake, potato salad, etc.). Eggs can be omitted completely if protein from other sources is included each day.
- Legumes, nuts (preferably peanuts) and seeds as ingredients in meatless meals or as one snack a day (one portion or a handful).
- Two to four slices of whole grain bread a day, or the equivalent of other whole grain foods (cereal, brown rice, brown noodles, etc.).
- Two to four glasses of skim or 1 percent or 2 percent

milk daily, or the equivalent (cottage cheese, yogurt, ice milk, and so on).

THE GENERALLY AGREED UPON NO-NO'S ARE:

- Chemicals (*whenever possible* buy brands that contain no artificial coloring, flavoring or preservatives or those that list none of the labels.
- More sugar than comes in fruits, vegetables, grain foods or an *occasional* sweet treat. Avoid the sugar that comes tucked away as a minor ingredient in unlikely foods such as catsup and bread. Read labels. Whenever possible, buy fresh foods, or canned and frozen foods *without* added sugar.
- More calories than come in the *amount* of food recommended. You won't put on weight eating bread, etc., if you eat no more than amounts suggested.
- More cholesterol than comes in the recommended foods above.
- More salt than goes into canned, frozen and restaurant food. Many cooks no longer use salt in cooking and baking, and their eaters don't even know it. Don't mention it. Keep salt off the table. Encourage your eaters to salt only those few foods that they think urgently need salt. Do not buy salted snack foods.

Fourth, Making an "Eat More" and an "Eat Less" List for Each Converting Person—A Personal Prescription

We make and review this list with the child five years old or older (including teenagers) and with mates, colleagues, the children in our class, or others converting with us. We review our own records. It's vital to the success of this project to comment with pleasure on each category of food which we are already properly eating or avoiding. Each person's Eat More—Eat Less List is his or her individual prescription.

Fifth, Making a Personal Poster

Each person now copies, enlarged to poster size, the graph conversion chart at the end of this book. He may want to decorate the poster gaily. Contrary to popular opinion, eating nutritiously need not be grimly done. Adults or teenagers with artistic talent may want to make posters for very young children. Students in higher grades may be enlisted as assistants to aid lower grade teachers with this part of the project (or any part!). Making a food conversion poster for each student would be a great activity for the art teacher to sponsor.

Sixth, Giving Each Person a Head Start

Now, looking at one's own eating records, each of us puts a star in the poster column in which he or she *already deserves one:* in each and every food category in which he has no problems. In other words, we go to our personal poster, and *paste a gold star any place where we already "pass the test."* People should prevent each other from feeling bad if they don't get a star yet. Children should paste on their own stars. They should understand why they get a starting star, and why they don't. The fact that each person will have ample opportunity to earn stars should be explained. This is not to be done punitively or threateningly. Conversion will only work if converters find it enjoyable.

An Example of This Six-Step Process

Ten-year-old Mel recorded his own food consumption (if, in this case, it could be graced with that name) with a few kindly reminders from his mother who said that snacks were food, too, though Mel insisted they didn't count. Until they recorded what Mel actually ate, his Mom had been convinced that he "never ate a thing." Mel's eating record is an excellent illustration of why some children aren't hungry at meals, are "choosey" at dinner time, and behave badly at the table. It is also exhibit A of the much-fed, malnourished "spoiled" yet uncared for American child.

Here's what Mel ate in a typical day:

7:30 A.M.　　BREAKFAST
Two bowls of sugar-frosted cereal flakes with whole milk. (There are cereals *without* sugar coatings. Skim milk is preferable since whole milk contains unnecessary calories and cholesterol. Any milk is better than no milk, but 1 percent or 2 percent would be even better.)

8:30 A.M.　　Four packaged coconut cookies (label lists five chemical additives as well as sugar as the major ingredient. Mother was in the basement ironing; Mel went into the kitchen on his own. His mother didn't know about this almost-400 calorie snack.)

9:15 A.M.　　A packaged fried-apple pie and a glass of orange soda. (She didn't see Mel help himself to this snack, either, though she did find the wrapper and say mildly that he shouldn't make a mess in the kitchen. This "little nothing" added another 350 calories, with a great deal of sugar, extra cholesterol, and scarcely any nutrition.)

10:30 A.M.　　Five chocolate chip cookies and part of a glass of milk. ("Now it's morning snack time," Mel's mother invites. "How about chocolate chip cookies with your milk?" She puts out two cookies. Mel whines, kisses her, and smiles winningly for more. Not counting the milk which Mel didn't finish, Mel has just consumed another 250 calories. The cookies were *not* made with whole wheat flour, and they *did* have chemical additives.)

11:30 A.M. A bag of potato chips (with BHA and BHT, and unnecessary fat and salt. Because Mel fussed that he was hungry and couldn't wait till lunch. Mother hates fussing, and as Mel triumphantly knows, always yields to it.)

12:15 P.M. LUNCH
Mother serves Mel a frozen beef dinner. (He eats half of the beef in the frozen dinner, and none of the rest of it. Had he eaten all of it, Mel would have consumed an incredible assortment of chemical flavorings, colorings, thickeners, and preservatives: water, cooked beef, peas, carrots, dehydrated potato flakes, margarine, cornstarch, vegetable oil, flour, salt, malto-dextrin, hydrolyzed vegetable protein, whey solids, monosodium glutamate, caramel color, sugar sodium caseinate, flavoring, dextrose, spice, celery seed, imitation butter flavor, cysteine and thiamine hydrochloride, and gum arabic.* Probably the best thing that can be said for this meal is that Mel rejected almost all of it. Because Mel "tasted" his dinner, his mother permitted him to have a desert, a "Ring Ding" of over 350 calories, gobs of sugar, and some more chemicals. His lunch beverage was fruit drink—sugar and chemicals, nothing fruity about it except the fake flavor.)

1:30 P.M. Mel is cranky, can't find a friend to play with, needs consolation. Mother says he can help her make a cake from a mix. He eats four tablespoons of inferior ingredients covered up with food flavoring, food

---

* Ingredients of a frozen beef dinner as listed in *Health Foods, Fads and Fakes.*

coloring, and preservations. Since this makes him thirsty, he downs two tall glasses of grape Kool-Aid—artificial coloring, artificial flavoring, and all.

3:30 P.M.   Mother sees Mel coming in from play and wanting a snack. She offers an apple and a glass of orange juice. Mel downs both, and also makes himself a "small" sandwich with two slices of white bread (not healthy whole grain), peanut spread (not real peanut butter), and jam with red dye Number 2 (the most widely used and highly controversial food coloring. There are plenty of jams on supermarket shelves *without* artificial colors and flavors.)

5:00 P.M.   The afternoon wore on without much more eating. Mel only had a few handfuls of Cracker Jacks, sticky with sugary glop and preserved with more you-know-what.

6:00 P.M.   DINNER

Family dinner. Mel complains that he isn't hungry and mother says to father, "That child has the appetite of a bird; he never eats a thing." But Mel does manage to eat some chemical-laden Hamburger Helper, drink a glass of milk, and eat a Hunt Snack Pack fruit cup, saturated in sugar and so on.

8:00 P.M.   While watching TV, Mel unwittingly put the equivalent of half a cup of peanuts into into his mouth—and the shells onto the floor. Peanuts are excellent protein. He also ate some salami, complete with dangerous sodium nitrite.

9:00 P.M.   He drank a glass of milk before bed.

Question Number 1: What did Mel's mother mean when she said he "never eats"?

Question Number 2: Why didn't Mel "eat"?

Question Number 3: If it's calculated that the average American currently consumes five pounds of chemicals a year, how many pounds can we suppose *Mel* devours?

Putting Gold Stars on the Personal Poster; Mel Gets Gold Stars?

Following the "think positive, be encouraging" thrust of the conversion project, the next step, while reviewing these findings with Mel, comparing them to the goals list, and making the Eat More—Eat Less personal prescription, would be to say, with *enthusiasm*, "Hey, Mel, will you look at this; you have two gold stars already! You had more than the amount of milk the chart says." (Mother would now make a mental note to shift to 2 percent milk—it tastes the same—no need to mention it to Mel.) "And you also had the three fruits scientists recommend!" (Mother vows to stop buying "diluted and additive" fruit, and to buy more fresh and dried fruit.) "So put up two stars, each in its own column. Now, which food category do you want to start work on?"

People Who Eat Small Portions May Get Some Starting Stars, Too

Edna's parents also say their child doesn't eat. "She won't eat a thing," they say. To them, only heaping helpings and second helpings equal eating. Edna eats moderately:

BREAKFAST:

½ banana (she leaves half a banana, but wouldn't if they only *served* her the half she *can* eat)

½ piece of toast with butter (ditto)

½ Glass of milk (she "wastes" half a glass; who can guess the solution?)

¼ bowl Cheerios with milk (start reading labels— Cheerios aren't bad)

MORNING SNACK:
apple juice
2 Triscuits

LUNCH:
½ hamburger on bun (many supermarkets routinely
   carry whole wheat hamburger buns)
4 carrot sticks
¾ glass milk
½ apple (that browning other half wouldn't be left on
   the table if you-know-what)

AFTERNOON SNACK:
apple
2 cookies
¼ glass milk

DINNER:
½ piece of chicken
2 spoons peas
½ slab mashed potatoes
½ dish canned pears

Observation: Edna *does* eat. And she eats nutritiously. She just doesn't eat on the grand scale her parents believe she should. Maybe, when she gets bigger,
her appetite will too. If not, she'll be one of those
healthier thin folks. Edna gets start-up stars for (1)
three fruits, (2) enough bread foods (it's up to her
parents to start buying whole grain breads), (3) enough
milk, (4) enough meat or poultry, (5) her daily yellow
and green vegetables, (6) not too much consumption
of no-no's.

Seventh, Using End-of-Book Chart or Poster to Design Individual Ten Month Conversion Program

Some people find it easier to start, in month number
one (the month we're in right now as you read, whatever it may be; perhaps schools would rather wait and
start in September), with the food category we've
found we're closest to "good" in. This way, we don't

have such a hard job the first month—we're half way home to begin with—and we avoid initial "entry shock" discouragement.

For example, upon reviewing her eating habits notes for the week, Monique discovered that she *already:*

- Eats three fruits a day.
- Eats two vegetables or more a day.
- Eats meat about as often as she should (but since a lot of it is pork, she'll begin to reserve that just for special occasions).
- Eats fish and poultry sometimes (she doesn't like fish, but will try to eat poultry more often). Perhaps she will like fish casseroles, where other ingredients than fish predominate.
- Eats eggs, but every day (it will be easy to eat other foods for breakfast half the mornings of the week).
- Eats cheese.

Monique does *not* eat legumes, nuts, and seeds, so she'll work at learning recipes that include them. She will introduce these once a week or so. She does *not* eat whole wheat and rye bread. Our conversion plan calls for choosing one food category per month (salt, sugar, meat; each converter selects his own) to try to set right. When Monique gets to whole grain, she will gradually convert from white bread. She drinks milk occasionally, but will have to remember to have one glass a day plus one serving of yogurt and one of cottage cheese (which she likes better than milk). She may get more milk into herself by putting it in coffee, on cereal, in soup, etc. It's still milk even if it's a minor addition to another food. Of course, she uses a lot of instant foods, eats salami, bologna, etc., and drinks soft drinks, all of which are loaded with chemicals. She also eats lots of heavily salted snacks, potato chips, pretzels, and the like. Shrinking the quantity of these no-no's that she currently eats will be her most difficult area to change. She'll take that task on six months from now, since it will be the hardest for her, and will first pick *six easy areas.* By then she'll feel confident in her capabilities in terms of converting. Months from now, she'll tackle whole grains, which will be as hard for her as the chemical category will be.

Other people prefer to begin by choosing the area in which diet change is most critical. For many people, this is the whole-grain area—switching from white bread to whole-grain bread, from sugar-coated, largely artificial cereals to whole-grain cereals, from white pastas and rice to brown, from using white flour for baking, gravies, etc., to using whole wheat flour. The reason some people like to start by changing to whole-grain foods is that it's not so hard (they still get to eat breads and pastas!), yet earns the changer a great many "points," because these foods contribute significantly to better health.

If the poster is being used, each person selects the label showing what she or he will work on *first:* in the first month, for the whole month. He or she pins the label in place, where the chart says 1st Month. If you don't have the poster, cut the labels at the end of this book and use the graph page.

Now, Get Ready, Get Set, Start!

People "playing" this "healthier life game" are supposed to eat what they're supposed to—almost every day. One exception a week *on each item* is allowed.

For instance, if a person chose eating two to four fruits a day as her first month's project, she might eat none or only one, on a day when her mother wasn't able to have a fruit selection available in the house. She might eat none another day when she was at a friend's overnight and none was available, or none during the first day she had the flu. Or, she might eat five during the last two days of the month because strawberries were in season and she passionately loves them. *These exceptions do not erase the fact that her pattern of fruit eating has become excellent.* Even without the choice of omitting fruit, *she still has many choices regarding fruit:* two or three or four servings; one or two or three or four *types* of fruit; juice or fresh or frozen or canned or dried; one fruit alone or several kinds mixed. She is not a choiceless prisoner.

Or, if a person chose grain, and was in the country for the weekend where the rural store has no dark bread (as is unfortunately often the case in country stores), he might have to eat white bread until he returned home on Monday. Perhaps a second exception would be made in the same month: a holiday, with pies and cakes in abundance, all from the bakery, and none made with whole grains. A third exception might be the night he was at a restaurant which specializes in delicious white French bread. *Still, on every other day of the month, he ate whole-grain bread and avoided white-flour baked goods.*

Conversion Project Rules

Rule Number 1: The objective is *improvement* in each food category, not perfection, so praise should be given for effort, improvement, and *partial success. Under no circumstances should a person be scolded or mocked for failing to progress without error.* Occasional slipping and backsliding are permitted in this game. The project is for people, not angels.

Rule Number 2: Prizes other than food (privileges, outings, objects, etc.) or of edibles on the "approved" list, that happen to be a person's favorites, should be given from time to time to anyone *improving and genuinely trying* in the new area and in keeping up earlier months' new habits. Prizes should be the things the family can afford. They may be little things the "winner" especially likes. Prizes may be tokens that add up to something great (a trip, or whatever the converting person thinks is a reward).

Rule Number 3: The grownups involved with the children in this food conversion must convert too. The example they set and their enthusiasm helps provide essential motivation. Through their actions, they also serve as models of desired effort and habit changing.

Suggestion: Converting will be easier, tastier, and more fun if all the children in a family, circle of friends, or classroom convert together, and if each has a personal chart or poster. If it isn't possible to mobilize the whole group, it's helpful to have at least one conversion partner. *Caution:* If no one else is interested, do not let that fact deter you; just go it alone.

After the First Conversion Month

Pin the upward-bound label showing the new food category of conversion on the chart in the *highest* empty cube in the current month's column. Write the food category in which a healthy amount of conversion has occured (in colored ink) in the cube below the top cube. We try to keep up the good work in the completed category and put a gold star on it if we succeed *reasonably* well (as well or almost as well as we did in the month when we were focused on it).

The difference between this and a diet is that a diet is probably dramatic and temporary, whereas this is hopefully gradual and permanent. Why bother with all this? Because → → →

CHAPTER TWO:

Kids Aren't Eating Up to Potential

Biochemical Nutritionists Agree—Many Americans Eat Dangerously

Today, many of our nation's best trained biochemists specializing in nutrition are busy in their laboratories proving beyond a doubt that we and our children *are,* to an enormously and previously unappreciated extent, *what we eat.* Scaremongers and food faddists are not the only one who are contrasting what we Americans are eating these days to the diet of "the old days." Then, we ate better because wholesale, basic foods were the only foods available.

The food that most of us eat today:

- Fails to enable our bodies to develop maximum good health and good spirit.
- Fails to keep us relatively thin—a prerequisite for good health.
- Fails to enable our bodies to develop maximum resistance to an assortment of diseases and disabilities (including some of the biggies, such as cancer and heart disease!).
- Actually poisons us in mini-ways, cumulative ways, dozens of times a day!

Ordinary people, parents, and many pediatricians assume that an abundance of proteins, vitamins, and minerals can be found in commonly available foods. So, they believe, there's no need to think about children's nutritional needs. Many pediatricians have been assuming, for example, that blood routinely carries needed nutrients to all the cells and tissues of children's bodies. But there are overwhelming, negating hitches in these assumptions.

First, how many people, especially young children, eat a wide variety of protein-, vitamin-, and mineral-laden commonly available food? Second, how many people, especially children, are aware of and avoid destructive foods, such as foods that destroy antibodies that are needed to fight disease? Third, how many people are aware of the toxic agents that come nestled neatly in the "wide-variety of commonly available foods" they buy? How many know how to avoid food with these toxins? Fourth, how many people know how to prepare foods for themselves and their children in ways that guarantee that the nutrients remain in them long enough to get into the cells that will not thrive without them? Finally, how many parents and teachers know how to compete in a friendly way (not in a withholding and punitive manner) with "bad" edibles? How many of us can compete with, counteract, and *win* over TV promotion, friends' eating habits, and so on?

In all of nature—in the animal kingdom as well as among plants—living creatures are limited not only by the amount of food they get, but also by its quality and balance. . . . How about human beings? Are they apart from all the rest of nature in this respect? When we choose food at a supermarket or restaurant, is this food of *optimal* quality? Do all the cells in our bodies always get an *optimal* assortment of all the nutrients—minerals, amino acids, and vitamins—that they need? *

Good Nutrition for Maximum Freedom, Peace, and Creative Coping

A healthy childperson has more freedom, more peace of mind, and more ability to cope creatively with the frustrations of socialization, interpersonal relationships, employment, learning, loving, and life in general than

* Williams, Roger J. *Nutrition Against Disease,* New York Publishing Corp., 1971, p. 28.

an unhealthy or minimally healthy child. Parents who are not concerned with developing the child's various potentials to the maximum feasible extent will not need to devote time to developing a nutritiously sound lifestyle within the home. The same is true of teachers in the classroom. As we well know, we can eat poorly and get along okay.

But, without excellent nutrition, people do not have maximal vigor, resistance to colds and other common debilities, maximal intelligence, maximal good mood, and maximal protection against the major killers of mid- and later life (heart diseases, cancer, etc.). It is true that there is no evidence that good nutrition cures or even prevents cancer, heart disease, arthritis, mental illness, alcoholism, aging, or slowed intellect. However, there is abundant evidence that excellent nutrition leads to "maximally feasible" resistance to undesirables—illness, fatigue, etc.—and to the development of desirables—such as energy and clear thinking. *As researchers become increasingly interested in the relationship between regular eating habits and health, we will see more and more evidence regarding the dangers of poor diet.*

Good nutrition won't gain us eternal life. Regardless of how purely we eat and educate our children to eat, none of us, unfortunately, will achieve eternal life or perfect health. Aiming at totally pure eating is therefore neither worth the neurosis which frantic over-anxious focus on nutrition can incur nor the resulting nutritional rebelliousness our children will exhibit. But, eating much more sensibly than most modern Americans do is not impossible. It does not require ridiculous concentration to the exclusion of other interests and pleasure in food. Statistics show that within the individual context of each person's genetics and environment, sensible eating yields better health.

Eating in Relation To Becoming a Person

Having a casual attitude toward young children's eating habits is best. This prevents eating (nutrition) from becoming a battlefield of wills and a constellation of power plays that can lead the child to rebellious self-destruction. A child may refuse to eat properly in order to get revenge on controlling parents and teachers. *However, although a casual attitude is recommended, this does not mean that what young children eat is of little consequence.* In any area of childraising, parents and teachers may be excessively anxious and authoritarian. They may be excessively and absurdly permissive. Or, they may choose the well thought-through, moderate approach. The firm but not bossy approach to children's nutrition is the one strongly recommended here.

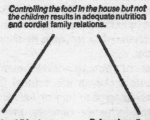

Controlling the food in the house but not the children results in adequate nutrition and cordial family relations.

Overcontrolling what the child eats usually results in eating problems, other behavior problems, poor nutrition, and hostile interpersonal relations.

Being absurdly permissive about what the child eats results in dangerously poor nutritional habits which are likely to be lifelong. Parents with this attitude shrug their shoulders and say "Well, what can you do? Nowadays, everything you eat is poison." Or, "It doesn't matter, they only eat a tiny amount of these junk foods and chemicals."

It's Safe (and Best) for Young Children To Choose What They Eat Only If Parents Are Doing Their Homework

Living cells, of which our bodies are made, are involved in a constant process of converting the nutrients provided them into the energy and special materials they need to perform their special functions in our bodies.

Those functions, as well as the efficiency with which a cell or a group of cells carries them out, are determined primarily both by the cell's inheritance and by the amount and quality of available nourishment. Although the upper limits of how well a given cell may perform its functions—multiplication, the manufacture of specific proteins and amino acids, and what not—may be established by hereditary and other factors, those limits are seldom even approached in nature.*

Failure of the cells to achieve top performance is consistent with other aspects of human potential. Few of us develop our bodies to the fullest possible degree—reaching our real limits—as fine dancers and athletes do. Few of us sharpen and hone our brains so that we use all of our "intelligence quotient." Few of us refine our interpersonal skills to the maximally feasible extent in terms of peace and love. In all aspects of our being, it appears that what we need is not more potential; *what we urgently need is to learn methods of developing this potential.*

In *all* areas of human development, a person's individual genetic make-up is a critical factor in determining what can happen to him or her. But, while average parents can't influence genetics, they can influence environmental factors. Environmental factors are extremely important in determining a child's personal destiny.

Healthy Cells for Healthy Lives

Cells in each person's vital organs—the nerves, brain, liver, lungs, heart, blood vessels, kidneys, intestines, glands, muscles, and skin—must be well nourished if we are to lead long and healthy lives.

When discomforts of varying degrees are plaguing us, it may be that our cells are hungry for certain nutrients and are malfunctioning, limping along performing their functions in a lackadaisical fashion. Or, they may be mildly poisoned. For example, if the liver isn't getting the nutrients it needs, it can't produce the more than *1,000* (!) kinds of enzymes it's supposed to for

---

* Williams, Roger J. *Nutrition Against Disease,* p. 30.

purposes of purifying and replenishing our blood. When
this happens, poisons remain in our blood, we feel below par, and we get minor infections, headaches, depression, indigestion, constipation, aches, and pains. If
we deprive the liver too much, cells die (cirrhosis),
and we do too. All our organs are linked together. If
the liver can't protect the heart from poisons, the heart
is in danger.

Study after study by respectable scientists and scientific organizations has shown that Americans have a
"poor" diet, lacking in:

• Vitamins,
• Minerals,
• Fiber and bulk;
Our "poor" diet also:
• Is too rich; that is, it contains too many calories
  (leading to obesity);
• Includes too much animal fat;
• Contains too many chemicals (food flavors, colors,
  and preservatives, and others);
• Has too much salt; and
• Has enormously much too much sugar.

According to the National Academy of Sciences, a
"poor" diet is one with less than two thirds of the Recommended Daily Allowance (which the Academy sets)
for each nutrient. Many American children eat a poor
diet. To make matters worse, the poor diet is soaked
in sugary soft drinks.

Why We Eat So Poorly

Some people are poorly nourished because they are
poor. Food costs money. While the rural poor may be
able to raise much of their food, the urban poor cannot. Until people are provided with opportunities to
earn money for food or are given food and receive
effective nutrition education, they will not be well-
nourished. Information about good nutrition is not
enough. As the noted anthropologist, Margaret Mead,

has pointed out, people don't eat nutrition information; they eat food.

Other people are poorly nourished because they eat too much of the wrong foods, usually sugar foods, starches, salt, fats, or alcohol. They become obese or alcoholic or both—or head for other nutrition-related trouble such as hypertension.

A third group of people lack a particular nutrient because of food faddism, ethnic eating habits, or nutritional ignorance combined with erroneous information generously provided by misleading advertising and the faulty eating habits with which parents and schools have unnoticingly let them grow up.

Minimum daily requirements are minimum. Recommended daily allowances come closer to spelling out nutrients we need. *Only parents can put "recommended daily allowances" in the refrigerator, on the shelves, and on the table—temptingly and exclusively. For, if "recommended daily allowances" share shelves and table space with non-nutritious or detrimental foods, any parent knows which food the children will choose!*

We parents worry when the teacher tells us our children aren't working "up to potential." Teachers don't approve of that. Well, very few of our children are *eating* up to potential, either. What about that? We teachers worry about the "junk food junkies" munching all around us. What can be done in the classroom? In the lunchroom? Only teachers, other school personnel, and people interested in schools can help schools get rid of no-no foods and provide exciting nutritious foods.

What Can Teachers and Parents Do?

It's very hard to raise and educate children well. But there are some things we *can* do, relating to the development of health:

• Eat right while pregnant.
• Teach children the importance of doing this, for they will be the parents of the next generation.

- Help children eat right in terms of the general principles and patterns reviewed in this help-yourself guidebook.
- Help children help *other* children do this.
- Teach children the no-no foods and how to develop strength in resisting them:
  —By our example.
  —By teaching techniques of staying away from tempting stuations.
  —By stating our confidence in children's ability to resist, in spite of temptation, without policing from adults.
  —By praising and rewarding children when they resist something tempting.
  —By showing brief but real disapproval when children make more than a *few* exceptions during *a week*.
  —By helping the child discover gratifying ways of spending earnings or allowances on itsems other than on candy, soft drinks, etc.
- Control the young child's eating habits by:
  —Stocking the house and school only with foods we know are healthy (healthy foods need not be dull foods).
  —Not putting "junk" food in his path between meals, while shopping, when we visit friends' houses, when we feel like treating, etc. Thus, we make sure the child is hungry for the healthy foods we have available.
  —Lovingly and merrily providing lots of treats and interesting foods that are *not* bad for people or, at least, are *less* bad than the junk commonly eaten today.
  —*Never* bribing babies, toddlers, preschoolers, and school-age children with rewards of "bad" foods (to stay in playpens, to eat more, to stop whining, to do their schoolwork, etc.); if bribes are essential, which they seldom are, there are plenty of nonedible bribes to choose from.

There are some other things parents and teachers can do, too. These things are important as well as what we eat:

- Create tempting opportunities for families and children to get exercise.
- Avoid smoking.
- Help create children who like themselves too much to harm themselves by smoking.
- Avoid smokey rooms.
- Avoid air pollution.
- Fight air pollution; teach children to do the same.
- Avoid excessive drinking of coffee, tea, and alcohol.
- Help children to do likewise.
- Avoid medicines and drugs whenever possible. Many medicines are chemicals unlike anything nature uses to combat ills; these should be used most guardedly.
- Help children do the same.
- Join consumer protection causes such as Consumer Federation of America.

While we parents, teachers and citizens protest that health is just about the most important thing, we eat to kill—*ourselves*. Our time is the scarcest resource we have. It's unreal in today's world to tell the average parent to go back to nature, do a little organic farming, and only feed the family fresh foods and homemade meals. Nonetheless, whether or not we're working urban parents, single heads of households, on tight budgets, pushed and pulled by pervasive, persuading advertising and intense peer pressures, or teachers who are assigned to teach subjects other than nutrition, still, *good nutrition remains a vital underpinning of good health.*

Americans believe that health is one of the most important things in life, and spend a fortune on it. But until we begin implementing at home preventive health principles, we can believe our heads off, and it won't do us any good.

Teacher and parent imperfections of substance and style are legion, but within the limits set by personal genetics, both natural and man made environmental forces, and an army of viruses and bacteria, each adult *chooses* his or her own degree of health and even length of life by the value he or she places on *preventive* behavior. Because the life you save may be your own or your child's, perhaps you'll decide to become a convert with us.

CHAPTER THREE:

Thin Is In

Growing Up Nourished-Yet-Thin—For Maximum Freedom, Peace, and Creative Coping

Overweight people are generally not as healthy, happy, long-lived, and comfortable or (frequently) as popular as nonfat people. Since lifelong, so-hard-to-change food habits are conditioned in early childood, why encourage obesity in children? Appestats, the internal mechanism that regulates appetite as the thermostat regulates heat, develop in children when they are very young. The appestat encourages the child to eat more and more and more regardless of the body's nutritonal needs; or prevents the child from being hungry *enough*. Fat babies are adorable, but fat adolescents and adults aren't. In all things, prevention is better than cure.

Fatproofing a child, by fatproofing the house and classroom, gives a child a marvelous freedom to become happy and comfortable. But one has to battle off a thousand pressures to accomplish fatproofing. One does *not* have to battle with the child. Fatproofing a house or group program for toddlers and preschoolers is a behind-the-scenes activity. In fact, the best way to cause the child to overeat or to eat the wrong foods is to hover over every mouthful. *Excess anxiety in any aspect of parenting or teaching boomerangs. It never pays.* Food fads and diets for adults and children are neither necessary nor appropriate. In fact they're a lot of work, boring to others who have to hear them described, and a sign of peculiar oral and narcissistic focus. But foodsafing and fatproofing a house aren't neurotic.

To raise children "right," nutritionally speaking, we have to rid ourselves of some of the beliefs with which we were raised. One of these is the idea that a clean plate is the best plate. If we don't serve children more than they say they can or will eat, we seldom have to scrape gallons of dinner per year into the garbage. Serving small portions saves food (and dollars), and prevents fat from forming in children's bodies.

Another false belief we'll need to discard is that children will starve to death between the lunch they don't want to eat "enough" of and dinner. Death due to this cause is a rare occurance.

A third myth we must cast off before we can start feeding children right is that they won't love us if we frustrate them by offering only "Good" foods. Children expect guidance and protection from adults. As long as we *stress the positive* (tasty food, attractive food, a lot of nonfattening food, and fun with food), children will not be warped by our efforts to help them develop antifattening habits.

Why Raise Children Thin?

It's important to raise children moderately thin because a high percentage of children raised with an overeating habit have an obesity problem throughout their lives.

Estimates indicate that between 25 and 45 percent of all American people are overweight. Many of them are 20 pounds or more heavier than they should be, considering their sex, the size of their bones, frame, and so on. Weighing more than 20 pounds over what physicians estimate we ought to weigh is considered obesity. Thirty percent of all American children are believed to be overweight. Many of them are actually obese. According to some obesity specialists, 85 percent of our fat children grow into fat adults!

And although the diet industry in this country has

climbed into the million-dollar bracket, it has *not* been impressively successful in helping people lose weight *and see that it stays lost*. Dieters are famous for their high relapse rate. For example, Dr. C. S. Chlouverakis, former director of the Obesity and Lipid Abnormalities Service at E. J. Mayer Memorial Hospital in Buffalo, New York, says that only one fourth of dangerously overweight adults succeed in losing 25 pounds. Only five percent of those adults lost 40 pounds. Another obesity clinic found that two years after the end of the treatment, only two out of 100 patients had maintained their weight loss!

Well, so what if most fat children will become and remain fat adults? Isn't beauty just a matter of personal opinion? Unfortunately, even if you believe that fat is beautiful, good physical health and mental health both go with thinness.

Obesity Is a Proved Health Hazard

There may still be considerable question about actual dangers of additives in food. But there is conclusive evidence that obesity is dangerous. Says one pediatrician,

> What's bad about being fat is that it is dangerously unhealthy. It shortens the life span. It leads to a much higher than normal incidence of very serious disorders, including coronary heart disease, high blood pressure, kidney and circulatory disorders, hernia, arthritis, diabetes, gallstones, and more . . .*

This pediatrician, Dr. Alvin Eden, points out that fat promotes a sedentary, inactive lifestyle, which leads directly toward early death from heart attacks. He observes that fat makes people miserable because they feel and look unattractive. And, they are "discrimi-

* Eden, Alvin N., with Heilman, Joan Rattner, *Growing Up Thin*. New York: David McKay Co., Inc., 1975.

nated against and persecuted in countless ways by a society that considers fat to be ugly." *

Physical Health

Evidence everywhere indicates an extraordinarily high correlation between obesity and incidence of medical problems. More fat people get injuries and certain illnesses than thin people. Moreover, fat people tend to get *more serious* illnesses and injuries than thin people.

The American Heart Association says that obesity is one of eight factors that makes a person a high risk for strokes and heart attacks. Just being consistently significantly overweight, never mind obese, is believed to be a risk factor because of the extreme strain it places on the cardiovascular system.

The Heart Association says high blood pressure is closely related to strokes, heart attacks, and obesity. The more excess weight a person lugs around, the more likely he or she is to have high blood pressure and, the higher the blood pressure, the more likely he or she is to have heart problems.

The Heart Association considers increased blood fats (chloresterol) another of the eight factors endangering hearts. Obese people are more susceptible than others to the accumulation of fatty deposits which plug up blood vessels, elevating blood pressure. Fatty deposits result from a high level of cholesterol and triglycerides in the blood. They get into the blood partly because of bad eating habits.

According to the Heart Association, a fourth factor that puts a person on the high risk list is regular lack of sufficient exercise. Exercise helps build a strong heart muscle. But overweight people usually don't get much exercise because it's so hard and embarrassing for them to lumber around. Lack of exercise allows the heart muscle to become inadequate. This prevents optional

---

* Eden, Alvin N., and Heilman, Joan Rattner, *Growing Up Thin*, p. 30.

circulation of blood to the heart. Circulation problems correlate with heart problems. Exercise is essential to having a healthy heart.

The Heart Association also points out that genetics and family history, stress, and cigarette smoking are all associated with heart disease and heart disasters.

Heart disease is America's leading cause of death. Four out of eight causes of heart disease are diet-related. One out of five people die of heart disease. Statistically, this means that one out of every five children in the classroom, neighborhood, and pediatrician's practice will eventually die of heart disease, and 50 percent of *them* will die of diet-related heart disease. Fat isn't good for people. Concerned parents and educators keep this in mind and apply it to everyday situations each day.

Compared to thin people, obese people more frequently suffer from post-surgical and obstetrical complications, respiratory infections such as pneumonia, circulatory diseases such as phlebitis and varicose veins, kidney problems, and digestive disorders including gallstones, colitis, and ulcers. They have more gum and tooth disease because they tend to get gobs of sweets, which enable cavity-causing bacteria to flourish in the mouth. According to research, fat people are more often hit by cars, injured in school athletic activities, and hurt in falls. This is logical; they're slower, clumsier, and larger targets.

Psychological and Social Health

While a baby doesn't know she's fat, and while a rolypoly toddler has no social problems due to excess pounds, a fat child enters the psychological torture chamber upon entering school. Immediately or gradually, blatantly or subtly, he becomes the target of other children's teasing and insulting comments. The extremely fat child is "different." We all know how cruel children are to the child who is different.

Even extremely plump children may have problems, but pity the *excessively* overweight, obese child. Fat children sometimes become ingratiating and "goody-goody" in their desperate attempt to win friends. Other children do not like these behaviors, and tend to shun them. Or overweight children may clown around to get the positive attention they so badly need or to ease the strain they feel with others who have contempt for them. By elementary-school age, obese children often become embarrassed to undress with other children. They may be left out of games and physical activities— a major pasttime and route to status of this age group. Many find themselves social isolates, often the recipients of painful gang taunting.

By the time the child reaches teenage, obesity is a real tragedy. This is true psychologically and socially. The obese teenager usually has an all-pervasive negative self-image. Research indicates that fat applicants' chances of acceptance to the college of their choice are one-third to one-half less than the chances of their rivals who are not overweight.

Employment Problems

Weight is also considered for jobs of typists, file clerks, receptionists and secretaries, where the public might form an impression of the company by the employees on display. Employers seem to feel that fat people don't give their organizations an energetic and attractive image. A survey was once done that showed that the average fat executive receives less pay than a lean one and is less likely to advance as quickly or as high. Even the Army rejects overweight applicants and insists that soldiers maintain desirable weight levels. So does the Navy, which discharges excessively heavy members as unsuitable.

It obviously does not pay to be overweight. The hazards are real and devastating and no child should be forced to face them by growing up fat.

Most Americans Can Control What's in Their Refrigerator and on Shelves and Tables.

It isn't just the food that's *served* that matters. Children of a year-and-a-half are famous for their ability to climb up, onto, and into any place that food is kept. They're better at finding food pellets than any rats in mazes. Although the kitchen mazes that toddlers can master in search of food are more complex than the ones rats have to cope with, the pellets they find are less nutritious (according to biochmists who've done analyses) than the nutritionally balanced pellets given to rats, birds, rabbits, dogs, cats, cows, and horses in the form of pet chows. If parents believe nutrition is important, they will forego controlling the child's search for food (it doesn't work). Instead they will focus on what's on the shelves in the kitchen. Snacks or meals. . . . It doesn't matter; what and how much are the questions.

How many times a day people eat is not as important as is *what* and *how much per day* people eat. Many nutritional specialists urge three balanced, sit-down, sociable meals a day, with no snacks between meals. But many others favor two or three *nutritious* snacks and smaller meals. We can suit ourselves as to *when* we eat, as long as we eat better than most Americans do.

Nutritionists who say, "Eat anything you want," can still be found, as can health fad nutritionists who think careful eating is worth concentrating on many hours a day. But, on the whole, nutritionists have long been knowledgeable about and concerned with the processes by which bodies use food, what happens if they lack what they need, and what happens when they get too much of what they don't need; and are pretty well convinced that *exceptions are okay, but what one regularly eats does matter*.

Fat Runs In Families

Research has shown beyond a doubt that there is a genetic component to obesity. Fat *does* run in families. Some children are inherently predisposed to being over-weight. But, like everything else about human beings, *nature* (genes included) and *nurture* (the child's environment), both come into play.

Since young children are essentially homebound, and their boundaries away from home are determined by us, we control their nutritional environments.

Some children's environments make them obese before they're born! Their mothers eat too much while pregnant and create excess adipose tissues prenatally! It's alarming, it's sad, but it's gruesomely true, that a person's food habits *and fat-cell accumulation* are in large part formulated for life by the time he or she is two years old!

Currently, several research physicians are convinced that mothers who grossly overeat during pregnancy overfeed their babies in utero, and thus give them an irrevocable accumulation of fat cells at birth. These fat cells may be temporarily empty if the child or adult diets, but they are *there,* like deflated balloons, ready to puff up again when fed. Evidently, these excessive fat cells created before birth have serious consequences for the child all his life. It seems that thin and averagely heavy children do not experience significant changes in fat-cell count except before two years of age and during the prepubescent and adolescent (9-18) growth period. But fat children's bodies make fat cells continuously, even between the years of two and nine, and at a faster rate. According to some diet and obesity clinics, people who become fat after childhood seem to be able to reduce and stay reduced much more easily than can children who have been overstuffed throughout their childhood years. Those who have the most difficult of all are those who were ridiculously fattened up before they were born. "It's almost like fattening these innocent unborn babes for the kill," commended a pediatrician . . . "Kill by heart disease."

Dr. Eden says that besides genes, another major factor leading to overweight is eating habits, "which are established in the very first year or two of a child's life. Once they're firmly set, it's not easy to change them . . . When I see parents who have already allowed their children to start off down the path of fat, I urge them to make their stand *now* before there's no turning back." *

Getting Thin

This doesn't mean that fat children, teenagers, or adults *can't become thin and stay thin*. It means that it's much more difficult for them than it is for the child *raised* thin. In the first place, it's always tough to change a habit. It's harder to *cure* a problem than to avoid a problem. Worried parents and teachers of seriously fat children face a difficult situation. Without offending or alienating the child, they must get him to feel that he has a weight and diet problem, and they must try to interest him in changing. But this is a delicate matter! If we don't say enough, our comments run off the plump duck's back. If we carp and harp, the child turns off our incessant, complaining words as a nuisance. If we are forceful, we're likely to injure the child's emerging self-image, which is always counter-therapeutic.

For parents, stocking the house nutritionally is *step one*. Serving interesting but appropriate meals and snacks is *step two*. Trying to intrigue the entire family with the idea of a "converting-to-better-eating" project is *step three*. *Step four* is speaking infrequently about what a good idea it is for the child to work on developing a thin, beautiful body.

Comments such as these, *always said in a friendly, warm and supportive way,* seem helpful.

* Eden, Alvin N., with Heilman, Joan Rattner. *Growing Up Thin.*

"It's hard to resist a piece of cake like that, but I guess we both will, because it feels so good to have a handsome body."

"It's tough when everybody all around seems to be popping goodies into their mouths, but we'll end up being better built. Feeling and looking good will be a reward even better than candy."

"We'd like to eat seconds of everything, but one serving is enough. Sometimes, it's hard to remember that we'll eat again in a few hours."

"I know so-and-so's mother lets her eat candy every day. Probably she doesn't realize how bad it is for her. But we understand, so we'll try not to eat as much."

The point is to stress the positive. Any comment should include the concepts that:

(1) *We* (not *you*) will be
(2) Happier (not only healthier)
(3) And, "I have confidence in your ability and willingness to eat right."

For teachers, *step one* is getting all the children in the class interested in helping their parents understand how to stock the house nutritionally correctly, or at least to stock it less harmfully. *Step two* is encouraging children to bring or eat sensible lunches and snacks during and after school. *Step three* is carrying out a "converting-to-better-eating" project with all students. *Step four* is to work *very tactfully* with the fat child and her parents on the subject of this health problem. The teacher does this just as she or he would if this were a hearing or vision problem or any other health problem. Good educators participate in more than "ABC" aspects of their children's growth and development.

Appetite, Appestat, Anxiety—Nutritional Need and Neurotic Eating

Appetite is different from hunger. As every parent knows, children can demand food without "needing" it; without being hungry. We know that there are ways other than giving food to change a whiny child's mood. But, we take the easy way out by providing "hush-up" food. The easy way out—and the road to poor nutrition, health, and appearance—is paved with lollipops, cookies, candy, potato chips, and crunchies and munchies of every manufactured, chemical variety. (A four-year-old we know once looked shocked when given a carrot and said, "Do *I* have to eat *real* food?") We do not have to yield to every request for food. Or, if we choose to yield, we can comply, but with nutritious foods instead of with junk foods.

Eating is natural. It does not have to be learned. Eating *enough* is natural. It does not have to be learned, or insisted upon, either. But *eating healthily is learned. It does not come naturally.* Especially in a culture such as ours, in which incredible amounts and kinds of junk foods and chemical foods are available to children. Parents and teachers interested in giving children the freedom and strength of good health will teach their children how to eat.

Fortunately, nature is on our side, so we don't have to make a misery of family life and a shambles of interpersonal relations within it, in order to get our children to eat. Children, like all members of the animal kindom, have a desire to eat. They have appestats that let them know when they're hungry and when they've had enough—

- *Unless* their appestats are biologically on the blink and they eat too much or alarmingly too little (eating too little is a *very* infrequent occurence);
- *Unless* they are so desperate to retaliate for excess parental control that they strike back by gorging or refusing food;
- *Unless* they are excessively lonely and anxious and fill their inner recesses—where love and security should lie—with food;
- *Unless* eating is a parent's major anxiety area, in which case it may also be the child's; and

- *Unless,* as most often happens, parents are lazy and stock up and cook with the wrong foods.

The child's appestat will work correctly when parents prevent overeating and poor eating by stocking up with and cooking foods that are nutritious.

Nature is on our side in another way, too. In America, there is an abundance of plants and animals which can fill our cells' nutritional needs. The right food is here. All we have to do is stock our shelves properly, cook and serve these foods attractively, and prevent children from filling themselves with sugar-laden foods before nourishing meals and snacks.

It's conceivable that some children are born with faulty appestats which do not tell them when to stop eating. Any other body part can be born defective; why not an appestat? But most people, once having attained adulthood, remain relatively the same weight all their lives, though they never count calories and don't weigh themselves constantly. This is because, averaged out over a week, year after year, they usually eat the same amount. Something invisible regulates their food intake. It's doubtful that *many* babies are born with defective appestats. It seems much more likely that they're born with defective parents. This parental defectiveness is being overcome today as parents realize how dangerously we've been letting our children eat. Teachers have been negligent too. Teachers are supposed to guide children's behavior and attitudes.

Many obesity experts are convinced that psychological problems—in other words, interpersonal problems between parent(s) and child—are at the root of chronic obesity.

"Obese people are neurotic," Theodore Rubin, M.D., points out. "Neurosis is a basis of obesity, which is the emotional state of mind leading to overeating. Obesity makes for more neurosis. Obese people—as long as they are without insight—remain overweight and fat. Of course insight alone will not cure obesity. It is also essential to eat less.

"Fatness, like all other aspects of neuroses, promotes impaired ways of relating to oneself, to others, and to one's work. Obese people are cut off from themselves and other people by the same psychology that produces a wall of fat. Obesity and overweight always have a destructive effect, both physically and psychologically. . . . Obese people suffer much misery. . . . Obesity in fact = misery." *

Fat Psychology

Apparently, people who are obese (more than 10 percent, or, in adulthood, 20 pounds over the normal, medically accepted weight for their size) suffer from *fat psychology* as well as biological problems related to fatness.

Fat psychology includes:

- Preoccupation with food and/or weight. (People with ordinary psychology regarding food don't think *excessively* about food, about what they eat, or about weight.)
- Food addiction, accompanied by *regularly* eating too much of whatever is eaten. (People with ordinary food psychology don't eat excessively in terms of frequency or quantity. Nor do they use "will power." They just stop eating when, from a nutritional view point, their bodies have enough food.)

Food addiction is a phenomenon familiar to obesity experts.

"It is virtually impossible for the obese person to eat just a little food—to take just a taste of something —when still more is available," Dr. Rubin says.

Most food addicts are addicted to particular foods. Many are vulnerable to sweet foods, especially chocolate. Many of these people respond to food like some alcoholics to alcohol. "They can abstain from chocolate sometimes even when it is present in the same room

* Rubin, Theodore Isaac. *Forever Thin*. Bernard Geis Associates. (No city or date given on book.) pp. 30-32.

with them. But should the addict taste—merely taste—
the addicting food, an overwhelming and insurmount-
able 'need' for the food in question will be initiated. His
mouth hunger at this time will become unbearable, and
he will feel that it can be relieved only by huge quantities of the 'offending' substance," Dr. Rubin says.*

Excess Anxiety Can Cause Food Addiction

Children do not need to live in families of fat people
to develop neurotic eating habits, gluttonous appetites,
or addictions to specific foods. For example, excessively
anxious children are particularly prone to neurotic behavior (behavior intended to allay excess anxiety),
which may easily and often does take the form of undesirable eating habits. These are

1) Lonely, insecure children,
2) Especially angry children, or
3) Children whose parents are excessively anxiety-
   ridden (full of inner conflict, ambivalence, and
   unresolved conscious and unconscious problems
   of their own).

Often, such parents are so preoccupied with themselves that they don't "see" what their children eat. Or,
they are so ambivalent about setting limits that they
overpermissively allow their children to eat absurdly
(although upon occasion they may "notice" and suddenly, temporarily, curb certain kinds of eating).

Children who consciously or unconsciously feel un-
loved, less loved than a brother or sister, rejected, or
emotionally deprived tend to eat and eat, using food
symbolically to fill themselves and to allay anxiety.
Since food gets to the pit of the stomach and not to the
emotional roots of the anxiety, it doesn't allay anxiety.
The eater has to eat more and more, in everlasting
hope of eating "enough." Even if parents of these children try extremely hard to govern the child's overeat-

* Rubin, Theodore Isaac. *Forever Thin*, pp. 21-22.

ing, *and even if they use appropriate approaches,* they are unlikely to succeed. The solution isn't in the kitchen, it's in correcting the psychological situation in the parent, in the family, and in the overeater.

Children who feel that they aren't loved and are not noticed enough may overeat as a way of focusing parental attention on themselves many times a day. Children who feel retaliative and vindictive and who have power problems with their parents may eat excessively as a way of punishing the parents. Conversely, many parents use food to reward or punish children. Is this where children learn to use food as a weapon?

Controlling food and eating won't solve the problem unless the psycho-dynamics of the situation are solved too. Children who feel self-hate, perhaps unknowingly, may make food part of their problem.

"Many people eat in order to become grotesque and sick as a form of self-punishment. . . ." *

Coping Creatively With Excess Anxiety

From time to time, we all suffer from *temporary* excess frustration, conflict, and anxiety. Nobody is exempt from occasionally feeling nervous, tense, agitated, angry, or apprehensive. We may find it hard to eat at these times, or we may feel gluttonous. Children likewise. Eating seems to be one of a number of reasonable ways of occasionally coping creatively with excess anxiety. It may be a better way than attacking loved ones in fits of tension-caused rage. Being imperfect occasionally, in eating habits and other habits, can protect us from extremely irrational behavior.

However, eating abusively is probably a poor route for the repression of anger and of expression of the *chronically excessively anxious person,* because it leads to so many other problems. There are less punishing, less destructive ways to act out excessive anxiety.

* Rubin, Theodore Isaac. *Forever Thin,* p. 47.

Perhaps It Would be Better for Parents Not to Create Excessively Anxious Children

If our society placed a higher value on good mental health, we could help parents help children. As it is, our society offers little help to parents with personal or interpersonal or childraising problems, overeating or any other.

National emphasis needs to be placed on helping parents become better parents, if our society is to produce mentally healthy children. This emphasis is beginning to emerge. Even though our communities do not offer easily available excellent help, it is usually possible for a perservering parent to find some degree of help somewhere. In most areas of the country, there are county or city mental health clinics. Many school systems and preschools have connections with psychologists. Parent education groups are springing up around the country. Some hospitals, clinics, clergymen, and pediatricians specialize in family problems. Of course, there are private psychiatrists and psychotherapists as well. Teachers can assist parents in seeking and locating counseling services when a child seems to be in some sort of sustained emotional trouble with parents. Parents can insist that their child be transferred when a child seems to be in some sort of frequent emotional trouble with a teacher. When a child's obesity seems to be caused by psychological problems, it's wise to seek professional help from a psychotherapist.

Faulty Eating Patterns More Likely Than Psychological Problems

However, in cases of fatness, it is best to think first about family and child eating patterns. If all reasonable attempts have been made to correct these—just to "normal," not to perfect—and a strangely strong resistance to eating right is still noticed, emotional problems may be at the bottom of the problem. Or at the bottom of the belly, as the case may be.

A helpful environment makes available a wide variety of nutritious foods; minimizes sweets, animal fat foods, and chemical colorings, flavorings, and preservatives; and establishes the idea of eating small rather than large quantities from earliest childhood.

If parents and teachers don't believe the dangers of obesity are bad enough to call for more attention to better eating, there are other reasons for concern.

CHAPTER FOUR:

Living to Eat, Eating to Live, Eating to Die, or Eating Right?

Good Nutrition for Resistance to Fatal Disease: High Fiber Foods

We have long known that massive amounts of sugary foods are denticidal. But few knew they are also suicidal. Apparently, while helping children from infancy onward to develop positive self, self-image, and interpersonal relations, we can also help them develop protection from some of the most serious diseases of civilization. We can help them develop a healthy self by developing greater immunity from some of the terrible diseases that our society believes to be inevitable, but which are not inevitable. No matter what we eat or don't, and allow our children to eat or not eat, we will achieve neither eternal life nor disease-free life. The human condition doesn't permit permanent perfect health any more than it permits permanent perfect happiness.

However, according to David Reuben, M.D., who draws on medical research carried out by more than 500 respected scientists around the world and who is being taken seriously by increasing numbers of reputable physicians, a high-fiber diet, familiar in many parts of the world but unheard of in America, can offer:

- "Protection from the number-one fatal cancer in America—cancer of the colon * and rectum—striking 99,000 Americans each year;

* The United States has nearly the highest rate of cancer of the colon in the world.

- "Protection from heart attack—the epidemic that kills 700,000 Americans every year and ranks as the primary cause of death in our country;
- "Freedom from the symptoms of diverticulosis—the most common disease of the colon in the United States, affecting nearly half the population over the age of forty;
- "Protection from appendicitis; the number one abdominal surgical emergency, responsible for 200,000 operations and 20,000 deaths a year;
- "Real hope for overcoming obesity, the condition that handicaps 50 percent of our citizens; and
- "Helping in dealing with hemorrhoids, constipation, and varicose veins—those annoying and disabling legacies of civilization." *

Fibrous Foods Are Whole Grain Foods; Fruits, and Vegetables

High fiber diet means more roughage: more whole grain foods and more raw fruits and vegetables, with peel whenever practical. Dark breads made of coarsely milled flours with fiber and bran left where nature put them are cleansers to the colon. White bread, sweet rolls, doughnuts, "tasty cake"-type lunch box desserts, cake mixes, and ordinary pancakes, are not. Eating these refined-flour foods deprives us in two ways of the rougher grain foods we need:

- They don't contain the fiber we need.
- They fill us up so fast we have no hunger for the coarser foods that we *do* need.

Without being aware of it, each recent generation of Americans has been eating less roughage. Besides white flour, we also eat white noodles, spaghetti, and rice. Whole grain noodles, spaghetti, and brown rice are a great deal better for us in terms of roughage. They are

* Reuben, David. *The Save-Your-Life Diet.* New York: Random House, 1975. jacket

available at some grocery stores and at almost all health food stores.

At the same time that we've been providing our children with less roughage to grow up on, we've been saturating their intestines with more sugar: soft drinks, candy, cakes, cookies, pies, jams, jellies, and syrups. Sugar is an additive in nearly everything that comes in a can or package!

Besides filling the children's bellies with appetite killers that keep them from eating wholesome whole-grain foods, we dull their interest in natural sweets: fruits. Fruits are fibrous; the sugar foods listed above are not. Fruits are also full of vitamins not found in sugary junk food.

How many sweet-stuffed children eat lots of roughage-rich raw vegetables? Children who do not have junk foods available to them tend to snack happily enough on fruits and vegetables. Schools like to make rules. Absurd school rules abound today. Why not have a *sensible* school rule banning junk food and requiring whole grain bread, a vegetable, and a fruit in every lunchroom or lunchbox meal?

Fiber-Deficiency Diseases; Cancer and Heart Disease

Cancer and heart disease appear in large part to be fiber-deficiency diseases. Modern science has been very poor at curing these diseases. As a matter of fact, until now scientific focus has not even been on discovering the causes of and ways to prevent cancer. The Federal Government spends approximately $800 million a year to finance the activities of the National Cancer Institute. Of this sum, according to NCI officials, in 1977, only about 20 percent is for research related to the prevention of cancer. The balance is for research aimed at diagnosing cancer, finding cures for cancer, and treating it. As we all know, curing cancer is not one of our nation's most successful endeavors. Therefore, those of us concerned with the lifelong health of our children, will undoubtedly think it wise to emphasize *prevention*.

It is the concensus among medical and cancer research authorities that the overwhelming majority of cancers are environmental in origin. This means that pollutants in the air (including the smoke cigarette smokers inhale) and in the food, which bathe the cells of our bodies, provoke cancer. It seems that our ancestors were right that accumulating feces and allowing them to dwell for days on end in the colon—the result of a diet low in roughage—is bad for people. "Those on high-roughage diets . . . store their . . . fecal products in the colon for less than eighteen hours," * and are taking far less risk of the body absorbing dangerous substances. Doctors are quick to add that this does *not* mean they advocate enemas and laxatives. They're talking about the wisdom of eating grain, fruit, and vegetable foods every day.

The Deadly Combination: Low Roughage and Dangerous Chemicals

Dr. Reuben points out that, "Every cancer researcher agrees that cancer can be caused in body surfaces coming in contact with potent cancer-causing chemicals known as carcinogens." †

This includes not only the carcinogens in the air that we suck into our lungs via polluted air and cigarette smoke, but also the carcinogens we eat that cannot move rapidly through our intestines because of the lack of fibrous foods to push them on and out. Not only do we eat small amounts of conceivably carcinogenic chemicals in the form of all the artificial additives hidden in our everyday diet, but our own harmless body chemicals probably convert into cancer encouraging compounds if kept too long in the intestines.

* Reuben, David. *The Save-Your-Life Diet*, p. 30.
† *Ibid.*, p. 28.

Adding Fiber Helps Get Rid of Cholesterol

A simple, appetizing, and inexpensive addition of fiber to the diet can probably provide some protection from heart attacks. It works this way.

Most expert cardiologists agree that cholesterol is the primary cause of heart attacks. Cholesterol is a fatty substance. If it exists in too great amounts it clings to the walls of blood vessels and clogs them up. Cholesterol comes from consuming foods containing animal fats (fatty meats, whole milk products, eggs) and from the individual's liver, which produces it. We can lower cholesterol and still eat meat and dairy products if we eat, and make available to our children, only lean meats, skim milk products, and occasional eggs and if we eat and offer our children a roughage-laden diet.

Without becoming nutty, we can put more high-fiber foods in front of the children at mealtime, in lunch boxes, picnics, etc., and in the places they look for snacks. We can put fewer obstacles such as candy in the path between hunger and nutritious edibles. To date, not one single scientist that we are aware of has come up with *any* reason *not* to eat a high-fiber diet. One need not get fat on it. It isn't necessary to eat much of *any* kind of food. A little goes a long way.

Are Cancer and Heart Disease Deficiency Diseases?

Ever since Pasteur found that microbes cause disease (an idea that medical men at the time rejected flatly), American medicine has been microbe-oriented. That is, it is focused on the fact that some diseases are caused by microbes. Microbes have monopolized medicine's attention to the extent that physicians have failed to explore those causes of disease that are principally *deficiencies*. Many diseases develop because the body is deficient in something. Deficiency diseases are linked to faulty nutrition. After it was first noted that beriberi was linked to a nutritional lack, the medical profession hooted at the idea for almost 50 years. Then, a Nobel prize was awarded to the doctor who discovered vitamin B (lack of which causes beriberi). Rickets, scurvy, and pellagra, one by one, were found to be caused by a lack of nutritional entities, which were later named. Medical researchers and physicians refused to believe that the cause of disease could lie in food or lack of a certain type of it. Proof was produced by scientists largely outside the medical profession.

Today, it seems reasonable to believe that fiber deficiency may relate to heart disease, cancer, and other illnesses. Consumers may be the "scientists" who prove this by consuming more fibrous and fewer unhealthy foods and by falling in fewer numbers to heart disease and cancer.

The Unnecessary Diseases

Americans suffer incalculable pain, pay enormous medical costs, or die prematurely from such illnesses as diabetes, appendicitis, heart disease, tooth decay, and intestinal cancer. "These illnesses occur in epidemic proportions in Western nations and are caused to some extent by diet and other controllable factors," Michael Jacobsen a scientist specializing in nutrition, reports.

Most people believe these serious illnesses are natural and inescapable. But they are rare or totally absent in some primitive cultures. "In short, these may be *unnecessary* diseases. The unnecessary diseases are difficult to cure because they develop slowly and quietly . . . not like measles or the chicken pox." Jacobsen says. "As youthful cigarette smokers demonstrate, it is hard for people to get too excited about an unseen enemy that will not make its presence felt for twenty or thirty years."

Eternal vigilance is needed. The pattern, popular in America and other modern nations, of eating lots of white bread, saturated fat, sugar, and salt is safe and delicious in the short run. But it leads to gradual changes in the body and may finally cause a heart attack or tumor. "Recognizing the long-term ill effects of our normal diet (and life style), coupled with a concentrated effort on the part of the public, the government, and the food producers, would allow us to greatly reduce the prevalence and terrible personal and social costs of the unnecessary diseases," Jacobsen concludes.

CHAPTER FIVE:

Modern Times—The Era of Artificial Food

What About the "Chemical Feast" That Slowly Poisons the Body?

Most parents and teachers, involved in complex aspects of daily living, will not develop the fervent attitudes bordering on hysteria and authoritarianism that many food faddists exhibit. Even if we become totally preoccupied with the egocentric project of protecting our bodies from all impurities, we will fail. The world is impure. Good is always infiltrated by evil. Life always ends in death.

There probably is no such thing as a pure food, though there is such a thing as a pure bore. Even if we devoted our lives to finding pure food, the packages it comes in or the pots and pans we cook it in remain, to some extent, impure. Some packaging contains contaminating chemicals; some metals give forth contamination. There's a great deal of commercial gulling, exploitation, emotion, cynicism, confusion, and self-delusion about nutritional needs, food fads, food fakes, and food facts. And there is much that scientists still need to find out about food.

But there are some simple truths, leading to simple guidelines. If these guidelines are followed *as a pattern* (never mind the chocolate-coated, chemical-containing *exceptions*), those who heed them can be assured that they are creatively coping with one of the many problems modern civilization puts before us: to eat or not to eat any particular food.

Combining Chemicals: Russian Roulette?

Anyone half-aware of the possible cumulative toxic effect of chemical additives in food will cringe upon learning that there are 3,000 different additives used in food today. Heaven only known how many or which ones any particular person eats on any particular day, and in what (dangerous?) ways they combine. In addition to the problem of not knowing *which* chemicals will interact *how* in *whom,* there is the problem of chemicals suspected by scientists of being carcinogenic, *and* the problem of *known* carcinogenic chemicals, some of which we may be consuming.

The National Cancer Institute has said that even very small doses of a carcinogen can cause cancer. Not everyone, or even many, may develop cancer but it is not possible to identify who can or will, even many years later. Authorities say it may take fifteen to twenty-five years for cancer to develop. Thus, no one can establish the amount of a cancer-inducing substance that any person can safely tolerate.

Chemicals, Calories, and Cholesterol in Pork Products

For example, the nitrites and nitrates in bacon, sausage, ham, hot dogs, bologna, cured meats and smoked fish, *do* cause tumors and hemoglobin problems in animals. *Many* reputable scientists feel that they should not be used in the amounts presently used in our food (for coloring or for preserving), but that a far smaller amount (for preserving only) may be all right. Meanwhile, they urge us to avoid these foods or to eat only small amounts of them. There are brands prepared without these evils, but some scientists urge us to avoid pork products altogether because of their possible effect on our cholesterol levels.

Avoiding Artificial Coloring and Flavoring

There is *no* nutritional benefit, but there are big questions about the safety of artificial colorings and flavorings. Experts strongly recommend that we read labels and *avoid buying foods* (bread, candy, *all* kinds of foods) that list either artifical coloring or artificial flavoring. Red dye Number 2 is the most widely used and most controversial food coloring. Not one single food containing it, from red jello to red meat, is essential to our health. We can healthily, and easily, avoid buying jellies, maraschino cherries, and other foods harboring it. Good fresh food *is* colorful and flavorful. Artificial flavor and color are not required. Dyed children's vitamins should be avoided. And when the children need medicine, ask the doctor if children's medicine comes *without* red dye in it.

Preservatives

The problem of preservatives is a little more complicated. Food free from preservatives deteriorates rapidly. Some foods must contain *some* preservatives to be safe. Not all foods have to be stored a long time; many parents can develop the habit of shopping for certain foods frequently enough that they can avoid purchasing those that contain preservatives. There is also swelling interest in homemade foods. For foods that require preservatives, scientists may be able to find ways of using smaller amounts or less dangerous preservatives.

We know so little, except that both cancer and the pollution of our body's interior environment with food additives are on the epidemic upswing and may well be related. In the case of most foods that contain preservatives, it's possible to buy the same type of food *at least without*:

- Artificial flavoring,
- Artificial coloring, and
- Sometimes, even without preservatives

Therefore, parents may want to move in this dechemicalized direction, category by category (cereals, breads, meats, canned goods, ice cream, etc.). Without becoming health food faddists, healthy *foodists* may find it worthwhile to move away from buying precooked and prepared foods and begin buying and using real, raw, unprocessed foods that we can cook and more or less control ourselves.

Fertilizers and Pesticides

We cannot completely control the content of our food, though, because food still may be contaminated by fertilizers, insect sprays, dusts, and pesticides. According to most authorities, there is no nutritional difference in the effect that organic and chemical fertilizers have on the human body. Evidently chemical fertilizers can't hurt us anymore than organic fertilizers can. Pesticides are another matter.

The issue of benefits vs. risks has come up in every argument over agricultural chemicals and additives, but especially in relation to pesticides and herbicides. Experts seem to believe that the benefits of these chemicals are more certain than those of many of the other additives they must consider. But the risks involved in pesticides and herbicides also seem greater. The answer would seem to be in the selective, controlled use of the safest possible insecticides.

It's not simple. Our nation (not to mention the world) has an immense need for food. Organic farming can't possibly meet this need. Even now, *with* the use of pesticides, it's estimated by some agricultural experts that one fourth of harvested food crop acres (75 million acres of food; $20 billion worth of food) is lost to pests.

Studies done before 1973, when a ban on DDT went into effect, show that DDT accounted for about one third of the total dietary intake of chlorinated residues (pesticides of concern). Because of the ban, we're much safer in this regard. However, aldrin, dieldrin, lindane, and heptachlor epoxide occur in our food often enough to require reviewing by experts.

We ingest more pesticides in meat than in other foods. Nutritionists and physicians say Americans consume much too much meat, particularly fatty meats like those from pigs. Therefore, not eating too much meat is showing wisdom with respect to devouring cholesterol and calories as well as wisdom regarding excessive amounts of pesticides. Because pesticides tend to lodge in the fat, broiling meat on a rack so the fat drips off helps get rid of it.

The second largest source of pesticides in our bodies is dairy products. Avoiding these pesticides presents a larger problem, as we are encouraged to eat dairy products. Perhaps the best approach is to drink several glasses of skim milk a day, eat a small amount of cottage cheese, cheese, and so on, but not to get carried away. Root vegetables—those that grow underground, such as carrots and potatoes—are the third biggest conveyor of pesticides from plant to person. Pesticides accumulate in peel. Peeling root vegetables before eating them reduces pesticide consumption considerably.

Biological Controls Desirable

A move toward biological controls—the development of a system in which predator insects eat parasitic insects—is well under way. It will be a giant step toward safer eating. However, this method is not only costly, but, like the leaves of food plants after parasites have had their fill of them, is riddled with holes. The chief defect of this approach is that it's tricky to assure that the right predator is in the right place at the right moment to eat the parasite. Some species of predators don't survive in the climates their intended victims do and so on. Other methods of biological controls are emerging. Sterilization of the male insect is one. Another is the use of microbial insecticides which attack specific insects and their larvae with bacteria and viruses, yet don't hurt birds, animals, or people. Also, plants can be bred for genetic resistance to many insects and diseases.

Consumers unite! Urging and paying for research and regulations to remove chemicals from foods is a more sensible use of parental energy than becoming excessively anxious on the subject. As individuals, we can't do research on additives, insecticides, and the like. But we can join forces with those pressing for increased government intervention in behalf of the consumer. *Listing* additives on the labels isn't enough, although it would be better than the present situation, which allows many ingredients under many circumstances to go unlisted. If no legitimate need for an ingredient can be proven (and stated on the label), it shouldn't be permitted in the food. Even if an ingredient is not known to cause damage to humans, why put it in unless the choice is between safety and botulism or some other *real* danger? Unfortunately, the definition of "really necessary" can't be left to manufacturers, who seem to find extraordinary numbers of peculiar chemicals "really necessary."

Some consumers feel, somewhat stridently it seems, that their "right" to buy whatever they want with whatever someone wants in it, should be guarded. Others are too busy with aspects of their lives above and beyond food to go to the food stores with magnifying glasses to read the tiny print on the labels and scientific dictionaries to help decode the significance of the words once they figure them out, and with the large blocks of time which the effort will require. *They* feel that it's *their* right to be free to buy whatever they can with confidence that they aren't being harmed. Not everyone wants to become a specialist on chemical additives to food, but most people want safe food for their families.

CHAPTER SIX:

Brains, Teeth, and Gums

Nutrition and "I.Q."

"In a recent psychological study, young undernourished children were compared wih children whose nutrition had been superior. It was found that there were 22.6 I.Q. points difference in favor of the better nourished group," * Williams reports. Every effort was made to eliminate consideration of other factors, such as differences in the intelligence of the parents. It was concluded that the undernourished children not only lagged way behind in intellectual development because of poor nutrition, but also that their intellectual development was indefinitely and presumably permanently impaired. Some of the undernourished children were tested for seven years. There was no improvement.

It might be better if parents concerned about their child's I.Q. and learning did more to provide nutritious food and less to pressure the child to perform.

Nutrition, Teeth, Gums

Considerably less significant than attempting to protect our children against obesity, cancer, heart disease and other medical problems and trying to give them the benefit of the full quotient of intelligence with which they were born, is protecting gums and teeth. However old-fashioned it may be, some parents believe it their obligation to develop the health of gums and teeth too.

* Williams, Roger J. *Nutrition Against Disease*. New York: Pitman Publishing Corporation, 1971, p. 65.

Cells make teeth grow. Teeth are made by living cells. The health and vigor of teeth-making cells determines how strong and resistant the teeth will be. Cells are nourished by the nutrients in the blood brought to them. Teeth-making cells will get the nutrients they need only if we eat these nutrients. The healthier the cells that make and maintain teeth, the stronger the enamel and different layers of dentin on each tooth. If the body in general doesn't get enough calcium, teeth release some of theirs, thus becoming soft and vulnerable.

Some people say that what the child eats won't hurt the teeth till permanent ones come in. This isn't true. Permanent teeth begin forming five months before the child is born! Experiments have been done with humans which show that mothers who eat poorly during pregnancy produce chldren who develop poor teeth; children born to mothers who eat well develop healthy teeth, though heredity plays a part here as well. Experiments have also been done which prove that a poor early childhood diet produces poor teeth. Again, heredity is also important.

There are five things we can do to help our children have healthy teeth:

- Eat right while pregnant.
- Help children eat right (this includes restricting their sugar intake).
- Use flourinated water or obtain flouride treatments for children.
- Help children brush and floss teeth correctly.
- Take children to the dentist twice a year from the age of three on.

After the age of 45, *eight of 10 teeth extracted are removed because of diseased tissues around the teeth, not because of tooth decay! The health and vigor of the gums, which is largely determined by the life-long nourishment they get, in turn, determines how many teeth an adult will lose.*

Says Washington, D.C., dentist Fred Greenspan,

"Parents who let their children eat these giant amounts of sugar foods freak me out. It's not only teeth and gums that are harmed, it's the whole system, the entire long-term health of the body. Sometimes we see infections in the gums which are symptoms of systemic infections, but other times we see symptoms in the gums that *lead* to systemic infections."

Dr. Greenspan says, "You can serve delicious meals and snacks without sweets, except natural sweets like fruits. You might have ice cream once in a while—I don't see how you can eliminate ice cream from children's lives—and you'd let them enjoy themselves at a birthday party. But they can learn not to buy sweet junk, and much of the time, they can say 'No, thank you,' when others offer them sugar foods."

TV, A Pusher of An Addictive Substance: Sugar

TV is the worst enemy of the food-conscious family. Children should be taught that any time they ask for a sweet advertised on TV, they will be forbidden to watch the show it was advertised on for a week. This way, they will learn to enjoy the show, but not to fall for the addictive substances TV pushes.

Speaking of TV and its evil influence on children's food desires, adults' food shopping habits, and everyone's diet, we should say, wild as it may sound, that there is no valid reason for children under three to see TV *ever* (there are more constructive babysitters). And, there's no reason for children aged 3-12 to see more than one to seven hours of *selected* programs a week. Sitting in front of TV deprives the child of the exercise and fresh air which are needed for psychological and physical health. It deprives the child of engaging in reading, playing, creative arts, and all sorts of things that develop physical ability, knowledge, initiative, interpersonal relations, resourcefulness, and character. If the TV set is kept in an out-of-the-way spot, is rarely watched by adults, and is not assumed to be a regular pastime, parents can reduce TV watching without having a punitive attitude. Children simply won't grow up absorbed in TV or consuming the literally sickening "nonfood" edibles it endorses and promotes. Teachers can take an anti-TV position, too.

Teachers and parents further interested in this subject can join citizens groups which are trying to improve the quality of children's TV programming and to reduce and regulate advertising on children's program. You will find you are not alone in your concern!

CHAPTER SEVEN:

Health Care Includes
Good Nutrition

Why Family Physicians Don't Emphasize Prevention

Only a few generations ago, sufficient nutrition was
not a problem for people of ordinary health and means.
People just didn't *eat* much sugar. No one put chemicals in every can of food, and so on. Chemical and
other food additives were unheard of. Even when those
of us now in our 40s and 50s were children, "artificial
eating" wasn't half such a problem.

Coping is becoming increasingly difficult for everyone. "A total of 2,764 intentional additives, for direct
usage, in packaging or pesticide use in food were listed
by the Academy of Sciences, Publication 1274, in
1965. In 1971, industry estimated that the number had
grown to more than 3,800," Dr. Ben Feingold reports.*

"The most basic weapons in the fight against disease
are those most ignored by modern medicine: *the nu-
merous nutrients that the cells of our bodies need.*" †

Developing a Sixth Sense—A Sense of Nutrition

The "new age" of consumer awareness is affecting us
in a variety of ways. One of these, for many people, is
a greater awareness of the food they eat. Many people
are beginning to realize how much "convenience food"
we eat, from instant soup to instant pudding. Fresh

* Ben F. Feingold, M.D. *Why Your Child Is Hyperactive.*
New York: Random House, 1975, pp. 126-127.
† Williams, Roger J. *Nutrition Against Disease.* New York:
Pitman Publishing Corporation, 1971, p. 15.

food, simply prepared, is becoming more appealing, particularly with people now in their 20s. Food that tempts the six senses—the usual five and the newly budding sense of healthy nutrition—is coming into vogue.

Thinking Through What We Can Do

What about *your* food preferences, fussinesses, etc.? What are you teaching by example? Think this through in detail. You may be amused to find that you're just as cranky and picky about temperature, texture, appearance, recipe, repetition or variety, time of eating, and the like, as your most annoying child! Probably, if you're a typical American, you eat much too much. And you may eat a great many more dangerous foods than you realize. *People who live in glass houses shouldn't throw stones! Converting to nutritionally sound eating* ourselves is the first step in helping the children. It's too much trouble to convert? Try our ten month conversion plan and *then* tell us: is it *really* too much trouble?

What was your parent's policy for handling children's eating habits and table manners? Do you see any connection between what your parents did and what you feel about food? Do you see any connection between the way your parents treated you as a child and how you treat the children in your care? Is your approach to nutrition appropriate today, or have times changed?

Parents As Partners

If you are a parent, what about your child's *other* parent? If the two of you have different opinions about handling eating and table habits, can you talk over your differences and arrive at a happy medium regarding your policy toward your children? If you are a teacher, have you ever used any of the ideas in this book as a topic for a group discussion with parents?

Nutrition and Normalcy Both Important

Deciding what foods to make available to a very young child and when meals and snacks will be offered is grownups' business. We need to consider a child's health, because he's too young to have judgment about this. We need to consider nutrition. We need, also, to consider a child's need to be "normal," to be part of a community, not to be a freak. It would be unwise to notice *only* nutritional health, and to ignore the child's need for normalcy. Even though our *emphasis* is on healthy foods, we can permit children, when with others, to eat approximately as the other children eat (perhaps with a few protective exceptions). Even if a mother feels strongly about health foods *as an eating pattern,* she needn't make her child into a social isolate by sending her to nursery school or a birthday party with instructions to the teacher or other mother not to give her this or that food (unless such food actually makes the child sick. Naturally, if the child has a nutritional disorder, such as diabetes, restrictions will have to be followed. But the parent can lovingly help the child to understand and accept such restrictions.)

The loneliness and embarrassment the child feels when placed in the difficult position of regularly not being allowed to eat what others eat will, if often repeated, add up to anger so great that it will seriously impair the parent-child relationship, and the child's personality. At the very least, anger can cause the child to refuse to eat (to punish the withholding parent) and to crave "junk foods" (withholding them so neurotically has made them a route to revenge), or to eat her or his way nonstop to obesity. The child may go farther and become retaliative in many unrelated areas of behavior.

Patterns Matter

The child's *pattern* of eating will very likely be healthy if the adult makes available a variety of healthy foods, serves food only at reasonable intervals during the day—*served in well controlled, scant portions*—and *helps the child see other foods as undesirable*.

Patterns matter. Exceptions, unless they are major traumas, don't. Adults control the choice. However, what foods to eat from among the available choices, is the *child's* business. What one feels like eating is a personal matter. Grownups have enough decision-making opportunities. Children need some. Even if eating is sporadic and faddy, the child will stay well. We can practice leaving the child alone on the subject of his eating habits, as long as the food available to choose from is relatively danger-free. Then, we will need to provide no signs of disapproval, no praise regarding what our children eat or don't from among the nourishing foods in the house.

Older children's food intake is much tougher to keep tabs on. Once again, however, the most important factors are those itemized on the next page, plus:

- Teaching the child the no-no foods and how to develop strength in resisting them:
  - —By our example.
  - —By teaching her techniques of staying away from tempting situations.
  - —By stating our confidence in her ability to resist, in spite of temptation, without policing from adults.
  - —By praising and rewarding her when she resists something tempting.
  - —By showing brief but real disapproval when the child makes more than a *few* exceptions during *a week*.
  - —By helping the child discover gratifying ways of

spending earnings or allowances on items other than candy, soft drinks, etc.*

What Children Eat Is Their Business, But—

Positive parents and teachers are confident that the child (from birth until home-leaving age) will eat if he's hungry and will eat what he wants to eat. They know that he will, one way or another, get adequate nourishment. *They will leave him alone* and will automatically convey to the child that they trust him. This is approval. As he develops *self,* adult approval will become self-approval. We control the young child's eating habits by;

* Stocking the house and school only with foods we know are healthy (healthy foods need not be dull foods).
* Not putting "junk" food in his path between meals, while shopping, when we visit friends' houses, when we feel like treating, etc. Thus, we make sure the child is hungry for the healthy foods we have available.
* Lovingly and merrily providing lots of treats and interesting foods that are *not* bad for people or, at least, are *less* bad than the junk commonly eaten today.
* *Never* bribing babies, toddlers, preschoolers, and school-age children with rewards of "bad" foods (to stay in playpens, to eat more, to stop whining, to do their schoolwork, etc.); if bribes are essential, which they seldom are, there are plenty of nonedible bribes to choose from.
* Encouraging maximum exercise (from creeping to running to active games) since exercise is closely related to appetite and weight gain. The need for exercise is a good reason for not restricting toddlers and

* Do you think you read this a few chapters ago? You're right. The only way to assure that conversion will work, is to drill these concepts into ourselves and apply them.

two-year-olds and for letting them get around quite a bit, for lots of move-around activities in the classroom, a good school sports program, and after school physical activities or lessons involving exercise such as sports, gymnastics or dance. Children should be expected to walk or to ride bikes rather than to be driven. This fosters independence and self-confidence as well as physical fitness. If the situation is safe enough to permit it, even six and seven year old children can cheerfully walk many miles a day.

CAUTIONARY NOTE: *Over* controlling the child's eating habits is as bad as over controlling him in any other way. It isn't appropriate to fly around furiously in front of the child, frantically purging friends' houses and nursery schools of all questionable edibles. The child will interpret this as parental interference with the normal pleasures other children are permitted. It will be felt as a hostile parental act. Anyway, *patterns* of eating are important. Sweets and junk foods *occasionally* handed out by grandparents, teachers, friends, etc., won't hurt. However, babysitters and other regulars must be trained. Fortunately, many nursery school teachers are becoming aware of the urgent need for nutritious snacks. If yours isn't, why not make converting the preschool snack program your project? One mother complained that her son "constantly" ate at the neighbor's house. It was suggested to her by another mother that she discuss the problem with the neighbor, or find more interesting activities for her son to engage in at home.

Like adults, children have food fads. We can let them have these, as long as their fads don't inconvenience us too much and as long as the fad foods fall within the *wide* range of nutritionally sound foods discussed in the following pages. We don't have to cater to children to be responsive to them. Spoiling is not synonymous with generosity and thoughtfulness. We need not cook something separate for fussy Freddie.

What the child eats, from among the healthy foods we serve is his business. Table manners are a different matter. What he eats or doesn't eat and how much of it he eats concerns only the child, *if it is selected from among nutritious foods*. But how the child behaves at the table affects all present. Teaching manners to the baby under 18 months means prohibiting him from exploring textures, qualities, gravity, and so forth, and thus is a direct contradiction of encouraging cognitive growth through use of physical self.

However, the very young child (18 months to three years) can gradually and *gently* be expected to learn adequate table manners without damaging his good feelings about his newly developing self. If his self is going to have to suffer to achieve table manners of a refined sort, he's better off eating ahead of the family, as a matter of fact and fun, not as a punishment, or with Mama's or Papa's friendly companionship rather than with fiendish criticism. On the other hand, if the toddler's immature messiness doesn't bother anybody, it's a nice family feeling to include her in the dinner hour.

Between three and five years of age, a child can be expected to learn adequate, if not refined, table manners, including not to talk when someone else is talking.

We Believe It—Why Don't We Do It?

Most of us are aware of and "believe in" the major facts of sound nutrition and in the simple methods of achieving them that are cited in this book. But few of us enforce healthy practices and patterns in our own homes and in our schools. Why?

Many meal planners have commented guiltily that they earnestly want to feed their families in the now-known "right" ways, but:

• "It's all so confusing, what *can* you eat? You're poisoned if you do, and you're poisoned if you don't."

- "The people in my family won't change their eating habits, but insist on eating what they like."
- "I can't think of anything to cook if all the dishes and menus I'm familiar with are ruled out."
- "It seems so bossy and stingy—it feels good to 'give' generously, 'allow' a lot, and received food-related love from the family for it."

Many teachers, from nursery through high school, deplore the contents of lunch bags and lunch boxes and the chemical snacks and soft drinks that teenagers constantly consume. But they throw up their hands, with a "What can you do?", and turn their backs on the problem.

There are adults whose nutritional permissiveness emanates from an unrealized wish to "blamelessly" retaliate and see harm come—through obesity, rotten teeth, frequent ill health, and eventual killer kindness—to the children in their charge. These people are knowingly or unconsciously hostile to the children they are responsible for. Other adults are in no way hostile. They are well-intentioned parents and teachers who haven't, until recently realized how dangerously we are all eating, or who've been given so many marching orders by the media that they don't know how to march except in circles or in place.

Ten Months to Better Health

For those who just don't know where to begin, the following is a 10-month gradual conversion plan designed to help individuals move from dangerous eating patterns to healthier ones, from where they are now to where they should be.

This is a gradual plan, because changing shopping, cooking and eating habits in rather fundamental and long-term ways takes lots of concentration and determination. It cannot be done suddenly. Those who insist on doing it suddenly make themselves so much work studying all the new angles, and deprive themselves of familiar foods so fast that they soon hate the whole idea, and go back to their self-destructive ways. *This isn't a diet.* Diets are a dime a dozen. It's a gradual shift in basic, permanent eating patterns.

It *isn't* confusing and overwhelming *if we begin to apply and get accustomed to one new principle and pattern a month.*

Children *will* go along with the project, at least in part, if it's *interesting, enjoyable, gradual,* and *generously done* and if it includes no carping, harping, heavy handedness, and hostility between parents.

Cooks *can* think of foods to serve if the conversion only involves *modification* of familiar dishes, drinks, and snacks, and takes place over a long enough period of time to become eased into new habits.

The conversion can be done in a way that's *more* giving and involving. There's no need for adults to don their witch costumes, mount their brooms, and be evilly restrictive. Of course, it's easiest to follow the conversion plan with young children. We can do it without their awareness, because we certainly control their lives more. Besides, habit *building* is *always* easier than *re*building habits. But school-age and even teenage people, with sound, self-caring mental health attitudes, will go along with such a project if it's tactfully and graciously done. (A child who is so self-destructive as to refuse to make a sincere effort at sensible nutritional care when tactfully presented with an attractive opportunity is probably in trouble. Professional psychiatric help should be sought.) Elementary and teenage people must be *included* in designing and carrying out the conversion. They must have a great deal of *personal power* to decide what they'll eat and what they won't. Or the conversion project won't work.

And everyone must understand throughout that perfection and complete purity are not the goal. *The goal is greatly improved patterns of eating in many ways on most days.*

PART TWO:

But I Can't Think of Anything to Eat— Suggestions for Making the Conversion a Treat for All

CHAPTER EIGHT:

Fruits and Fruit Juice Drinks

Specific suggestions follow for foodsafing snacks, treats, parties, lunchboxes and mealtimes. These ideas are based on foods commonly used by middle-class Americans. Parents and teachers can substitute ethnic or available foods as suitable. The same principles can be applied using foods familiar to any ethnic, racial, or geographical background.

Parents can introduce more fruit into the diet at home. Teachers can encourage children and parents to put fruits in the lunches they pack, the party snacks they bring to school, the car snacks car pool parents hand around, and into their food patterns at home. Parents can encourage teachers to be pushers: *fruit* pushers. Teachers can encourage *parents* to be fruit pushers.

Eliminate the Competition

Children (need it be said?) love sweets, and gravitate to them amazingly systematically. *If, day after day, there are not other sweets in the house,* they will usually gravitate to fruits. If the children are babies or toddlers, then parents and child-care programs have it made. If the children are preschoolers, it's harder. However, convinced adults can hold their own against four-year-olds. The older the children, the harder the conversion in one sense: their habits are already formed and have to be changed. Yet, in another sense, it's easier; children's love of achievement, competition, and self-management can be harnassed to the cause.

Children will *not* gravitate to fruits if fruits have to compete with chocolate, chemical and sugar pie, mix cake, candy canes, and 99 other types of nutritional no-no's. Attractively prepared fruits and fruit juices, covered over to seal flavor and vitamins in, and left leisurely in the front of the refrigerator, free for the pilfering, will usually be pilfered.

Make Nutritious Fruits Magnificent

The child's eating begins with what his or her eyes see. So the more attractive nutritious foods are, and the more prominently they sit in ambush on the child's hunger path, the better these foods can compete with the unhealthy edibles surrounding and bombarding us on every side. Unfortunately, most junk foods are magnificently good looking to children. Money invested in eye-catching bowls, pretty fruit plates, frilly toothpicks, fancy wrappers, glasses and garnishes, is money well spent. It's "bait" money. Fruit dressings, like salad dressings, add interest. The following fruit ideas are fine appetizers, desserts, lunchbox and lunch table specials, and birthday party treats, as well as snacks.

In spite of current controversy among nutritionists, they won't hassle us on this one. Anxious consumer ahoy! Here's one thing nutritionists agree on—they don't fight about the advisability of eating fruit! Worried about having to memorize all kinds of information about vitamins? Forget it; just serve a wide variety of fruit, especially lots of citrus fruits. As the kids consume them, you can assume that all sorts of vitamins are finding a good home without requiring you to major in food science. And all the following can go to school, to the movies, or on picnics and into backyards in baggies or thermos containers.

Ideas

Sliced fresh orange in pretty dishes with canned or fresh pineapple chunks and, perhaps, a spring of mint.

Little bowls of cantaloupe cubes, or other melon cubes, sliced peaches with fresh red raspberries or sliced strawberries in orange juice.* Or, instead of raspberries and strawberries, unpeeled apples, red or yellow pears, plums, tangerines, or red bing cherries. (Leaving well-washed peel on fresh fruit provides fiber, a necessity for maximal health of the intestines.) †

Pretty dishes full of applesauce or apricot sauce— sprinkled with cinnamon.

Bowls of assorted dried fruits.

Small plates of the following, with or without a sprinkling of bran or wheat germ for crunch and added flavor:

Apple, carrot, and orange with a little mayonnaise, sprinkled with coconut.**‡

Grapes, cantaloupe or other melon and lime juice.

Apple, celery, walnuts and mayonnaise.

Crushed or chunk pineapple, shredded carrot, and raisins with mayonnaise.

Sliced bananas (or other fruit) mixed with cheese chunks (baggies full of this are fun).

Celery, mayonnaise and shredded purple cabbage.

Fresh or canned peach or pear half filled with cottage cheese, covered with French dressing, sprinkled with nuts.

Banana slices spread with peanut butter.

* Cantaloupe and strawberries have more vitamin C than most fruits except the citruses.

† Do not use artificially colored decorations such as maraschino cherries, unless you can rely on eaters to enjoy their appearance but to avoid eating them.

** Apricots have more vitamin A than most fruits. Cantaloupes and pumpkins also contain A.

‡ If on a cholesterol or calorie diet, omit coconut.

A banana, cut in half lengthwise, covered with cream cheese and rolled in nuts (or French dressing, if desired).*

Cream cheese-stuffed prunes.

"Shishkefruit:" Banana slices, slightly baked and cubed yams or sweet potatoes, apple cubes, dried apricots, and pineapple chunks on skewers (or slices of any other assorted fruits).

Bananas brushed with molasses, baked, sprinkled with cinnamon and nutmeg, and garnished with lemon slices.

Banana rounds baked with a slice of cheese on top, and paprika added for appeal.

Raw unpeeled apple chunks rolled in cinnamon sugar.†

Fresh pineapple rounds or triangles.

Dressings fancy up all sorts of fruits. Try a pretty dish of various fruits (experiment with *which* fruits) drenched in these dressings:

Mint and pineapple juice.

French dressing.

Evaporated milk with corn oil, lime juice and a little sugar.

Lemon juice and confectioners sugar.

Canned fruit cocktail is quite a favorite with children, but throw out the cherry (which is dyed red) and sub-

---

* If watching weight (grownup's or child's), skip the mayonnaise and cream cheese on some of these. Cottage cheese or yogurt might be used instead. And eat no more than half a banana. Also avoid more than two or three cherries, grapes, bites of watermelon, or dried fruit—these fruits contain a lot of sugar.

† Yes, sugar. Most nutritionists do not feel there is any need to eliminate all sugar from the diet, just to greatly reduce sugar consumption.

stitute a bit of red strawberry. And remember that canned fruit cocktail contains quite a bit of sugar. You can make a very fancy dessert by mixing cream cheese softened with skim milk and canned fruit cocktail. This isn't for the weight watcher.

Jello and jello fruit molds, though loved by many children, *can't* be recommended because of the high amounts of artificial flavoring, coloring, and sugar they contain. Twice a year is enough for jello. Fruit aspics are fine but they're more trouble to make. Homemade fruit gelatins are excellent. See your nearest cookbook; maybe you'll decide that making aspics and gelatins *isn't* too much trouble. Your decision will probably depend upon whether yours is a jello loving group, and upon how full your schedule is.

Here's the idea: Soften the contents of a packet of unflavored gelatin in an inch of fruit juice—whatever flavor gelatin you're making; then dissolve *this* in the rest of the juice *heated,* and totaling 1 pint; stir, chill till set. If you want a whip, whip the gelatin when it's semi-jelled. It will double in bulk. Whipped fruit gelatins and fruit aspics are ideal for desserts and children's parties.

To make fruit spreads and fruit butters, put intriguing combinations of fruits in the blender and spread the results on whole grain bread, toast, or crackers (raisins and coconut, dates and oranges; apple and fig, etc.) To thicken spreads, put whole wheat or soy flour, wheat germ, or milk powder in the blender, too. Children enjoy making spreads and butters. If someone hates one of these fruits, put it in and don't mention it. Friendly silence goes a long way in helping people change eating habits.

Teachers, how about seatwork and art work projects to illustrate each of the above? How about one bulletin board called The Fruit Board, or something clever the class comes up with? You could have "The Fruit Idea-of-the-Week." Being the "author" or illustrator of the featured fruit recipe, could become a real prestige thing among your children.

Try warm or cold apple juice with a cinnamon-stick stirrer.

A fresh fruit slice on the rim of any fresh, frozen or canned fruit juice, with crushed ice or ice cubes in it, fancies up the drink.

Freeze cubes of light-colored fruit juices. They are very exciting to young children. Kids love to put the fruit juice cubes in other juice drinks. For example, put orange-juice cubes in pineapple juice, or pineapple-juice cubes in orange juice. Even fancier, put a stick in the cubes to make healthful popsicles.

Because one citrus fruit a day is extremely important for everyone (vitamin C), and because fresh orange juice is light years ahead of frozen orange juice in flavor, it's worth getting a good orange juice squeezer. It doesn't have to be the expensive electric kind; a press will do. You can also use the squeezer to make tasty vegetable juices, but the electric kind is easier for this.

Helpful Hints for Skeptical Grownups

1. Without realizing it, teachers and parents tend to make *'just'* fruit sound very dull. Never let your tone of voice or words convey the idea that instead of having good treats or desserts, "we're only having fruit." When mentioning fruits, speak as if you had produced a much-wanted candy bar.

2. If your children are under a lot of pressure from other children who bring junk in their lunch bags or who trot off to the store to buy junk, etc., talk to other parents and teachers and try to organize a group conversion project. You'll probably be surprised to find that a number of relieved and delighted parents snap up your idea! (There will be others that will shrug you off, or give you all the familiar arguments for continuing to eat wrong. You can give them a copy of this

book or politely proceed without them. Who needs *them?* It's *your* health, and the health of your loved ones.)

3. Do not eat, or let other members of the family eat *in the house,* or let children in the classroom eat, competing nonfruit sweets. Simply make it a rule. Children accept rules from adults.

Fancy Fruit Concoctions

Many cooked fruits are excellent snacks or desserts, so nutritious as well as delicious that no one would think of saying, "If you don't eat your _____, you won't get any _____." You may want to serve:

Apples or pears baked with lemon, honey, and cinnamon.

Whole, cored, unpeeled pears stuffed with raisins, nuts, and ginger, rolled in lemon sugar, and stewed (use the juice, the vitamins have run out into it).

Fruit sherbets of all kinds (buy them or make them).

Spiced fruit rice pudding (see *Recipes for a Small Planet,* by Ellen B. Ewald, Ballantine Books, paperback, 1973).

Canned peaches mixed with canned dark pitted cherries, dried apricots, fresh orange juice and fresh lemon juice, and dark brown sugar—briefly baked and served warm or cold.

Dried figs and apricots soaked in cold water till they plump; cooked slowly in 1 cup of water, 1 cup sugar, lemon juice, till tender. (Serve warm with this sauce: whole milk, 1 beaten egg yolk, 2 tablespoons sugar, vanilla, yogurt, blenderized and warmed.)

Homemade fruit pies, pan dowdies, and tarts (leave the peel on fruits like peaches and apples). Make the crust of whole wheat flour. For those not in the habit of making baked foods, such as these, we nonkitchen-

oriented parents must add that it takes only ten minutes or so to prepare a sensational fresh fruit pie, not
counting baking time. (See section of book on whole
grain foods.)

Homemade fruit ice milks (see dairy product section
of book).

Here's a party appetizer and a party dessert:

Avocado fruit boat: Fill half an avocado with grapes,
orange slices, and all kinds of melon balls. Cover with
salad dressing made of corn oil, lemon juice, and pepper. Garnish with mint, parsley or cress.

Strawberry-pineapple freeze: Into a foil-lined icecube
tray, put the contents of an undrained 10 ounce package of thawed frozen strawberries and an 8¾ ounce
can crushed pineapple without its liquid. 1 cup strawberry yogurt, and ¼ cup powdered sugar. Let freeze
till firm. Put pineapple rings on top before serving.

Ice cream has cream and sugar in it, ice milk or milk
sherbet has whole milk and sugar in it, sherbet is made
with fruit juice, sugar and water. It doesn't count as a
dairy product, but doesn't have the calories and cholesterol that ice milk and especially ice *cream* do. Children
get juice this way, as well as a sugary treat. Pretty and
practical for parties:

Apricot lime sherbet: Mix together 3½ cups canned
apricot nectar, 2 cups water, 1½ cups granulated
sugar, ½ cup fresh lime juice; put in freezer tray, freeze
till mush, beat, freeze till firm. Serve in fancy glasses.

Some Sugar, Sure—But Look at the Diet Improvement Here

Many of the cookbooks listed on pages at the end
of this book give recipes for delicious fruit puddings,
pies, cakes, and confections. There's no reason to entirely eliminate "visible" sugar from the child's diet.
Everyone consumes a great deal of sugar every day

anyway, since it comes in foods naturally. Some people
say that "raw" sugar or honey are better for us than
regular sugar, but most nutritionists say sugar is sugar,
and honey is too; eat some, avoid most. So, we eat a
few desserts with sugar among the ingredients, but look
at all the "no extra sugar" snacks and mealtime delights
we've found! And even the few *with* added sugar:

- Do *not* contain harmful food coloring,
- Do *not* contain harmful food flavoring,
- Do *not* contain questionable white flour,
- *Are* loaded with fruit, whole grain wheat flour, and
  other nutrients, and
- *Do* provide needed fibre.

As a Parent or Teacher, What Are Your Choices Regarding Sugar Consumption?

We can let children down the amounts of sugar they
do. This is the overpermissive, unhealthy approach,
given the facts of life (and death). Or we can attempt
to eliminate added sugar entirely from the children's
diet. This is the overstrict and unsuccessful approach,
given the fact that if sugar is totally taboo, children
tend to defy, lie, and even steal to acquire sweets. Al-
ternatively, we can greatly step up our efforts to find
other attractive and tasty, less-bad, fruit filled sweets,
and to stimulate children's interest in making their consumption of junk sweets infrequent.

It's patterns that count. If the daily pattern is sugar-
less as opposed to *sugar*less, fruitier, and healthy, a
slice of birthday cake and a Coke every three or four
weeks won't hurt, unless, in some cases, the doctor says
it will.

Fancy Fruit and Educational Activities

One of the nicest desserts after a big dinner is shiny,
attractive fruit served with cheese, whole-wheat crackers, or nuts. Money saved on rich desserts and sugary

junk foods can be spent to join a "fruit-of-the-month" club or buy fancy fruit from a store specializing in fresh produce.

When we're looking for an educational activity, nothing is better for children of toddler/preschool age than helping to wash, stir, dip, count, measure, or arrange the snack. Parents and nursery school teachers have responsibilities and interests other than guarding their children's nutrition quotients. They don't have time for activities like these every day. But there are lots of fun and educational fruit activities if you're looking for a project, to do *with* children.

"Mickey Mouses" (as children call them): Put a half canned pear on the plate, round side up. Add two raisin or dried currant eyes, a raisin nose and mouth on the bottom end of the face, and two pecan ears on the top.

Candles: Stand half a banana in a pineapple ring, and add an almond on top for the flame.

Party balls: Stick toothpicks holding the following delicacies into a shiny round red apple—pineapple chunks, raisins, cheese cubes, dates or prunes, tangerine sections, and other fruits that come to mind.

Super bananas: A banana sliced lengthwise and loaded with goodies: peanut butter, cream cheese, raisins, dried apricots, nuts, coconut shreds, everything you can think of.

Strawberry boats: Fill chilled and emptied cantaloupe slices with whole hulled strawberries mixed with the melon you removed; trickle on a little French dressing.

Party Drinks

Eliminate soft drinks, fruit "drinks," fruit-flavored powdered drinks, and the like. Say, "I've just learned that they're full of chemicals and sugar and that they're bad for our health. I didn't know that before. Even grownups learn things. We aren't going to have those drinks anymore except once in a long while. I wouldn't be a good mother (or father, teacher, friend, grandmother) if I went on serving those drinks now that I know they are so very unhealthy."

Be brave, be firm. We are grownups and guides, not doormats to be walked on by our children's dangerous habits. Instead of "bad" drinks, serve other beverages as treats:

Strawberry float: Soften 1 envelope unflavored gelatin in ¼ cup cold water and boil till gelatin is dissolved; add 2 cups mashed strawberries and sugar or liquid sweetener to taste, lemon juice, and milk to taste.

Orange milkshake: Orange juice, more milk than juice —then it won't curdle—and ice.

Lime float: Pineapple juice, lime juice, lime sherbet, soda. Serve in a tall fancy glass.

Orange fizz: Orange juice, carbonated water and ice cubes served with slices of orange on the rim of an "elegant" glass.

Lemonade: With real lemons, sugar, water and ice. If you want it pink, add something that is *not* food coloring or maraschino cherry juice—such as grape or cranberry juice.

Banana shake: Beat together ripe bananas, orange juice, honey, vanilla and milk; or, better yet and very popular, throw 1 banana and 1 cup milk in the blender and let the child push the button.

Apricot cooler: To a mixture that is half buttermilk or plain yogurt and half apricot nectar, add 1 banana, nutmeg, and honey. Make smooth and creamy in the blender and serve over ice.

Lemon zip: Put 6 tablespoons of lemon juice, 1 cup yogurt, and honey to taste in blender. Pour over ice.

Purple passion: Blenderize ¾ cups pineapple juice, ¼

cup grape juice, 1 cup yogurt and 1 banana and pour over ice.

Earlier, we spoke of party ice cubes. Another way to make them is to half freeze fruit juice ice cubes, drop a large chunk of fleshy fruit in each, and let the cubes freeze completely.

Then there are the less exotic but beloved brightly cheerful drink favorites: orange juice and orangeade (½ juice, ½ water, ice, sugar), real lemonade, beautiful clear red cranberry juice and so on.

Handle Fruits Right

According to almost *all* nutrition specialists and weight-watching experts, each person should eat several fruits a day, one of them citrus. In addition, many experts think people should eat some fruits raw with peel. Washing is advised because insecticide sprays may remain on the peel. Raw fruits contain vitamins, especially A, B2, and C, which are killed when they combine with oxygen. Therefore, fresh fruit should be eaten as soon as possible after picking or purchasing. And, it should be washed *very* briefly and gently because vitamins wash off. Fruit should be peeled at the last minute or, better yet, not at all.

Nutrients are lost in freezing, canning, cooking, and drying. Sugar, and sometimes chemicals, are added during these processes. Therefore, raw fresh fruits are most desirable. However, they aren't radically better, and canned, frozen, or dried fruits are very good for people, too. In addition to vitamins, fruit contains minerals and provides bulk and fiber, as do foods such as whole grains and vegetables. Fruit is believed by some scientists to help prevent cancer of the colon.

Facts About Fruits

Fresh fruit juices have more vitamins and no chemicals, but frozen and canned *juices* (not what they call "fruit drink") are healthy too. Apple juice contains much less vitamin C than tomato, grapefruit, or orange juice, each of which, in the order listed, has more than the preceding one. Remember this:

Best: orange juice
Second Best: grapefruit juice
Third Best: tomato juice
And they're all great!

Prune juice is high in iron which is often deficient in American diets—especially in toddlers' diets. Lots of young children like prune juice (if bigger people don't laugh about their liking it) because it's so sweet.

Artificial flavorings and colorings are increasingly considered by scientists to be nonbeneficial, and possibly even dangerous to the health. When buying dried, canned, or frozen fruits or fruit juices, read labels and avoid those containing artificial coloring or flavoring. Don't despair, *there are plenty that don't.* Preservatives are a little more legitimate, but sometimes even they can be avoided.

Avoid fruit-flavored artificial drinks—soft drinks, powdered mixes, canned "fruit drinks," etc. They have few nutrients and gobs of detriments.

Dried fruits are tasty too. Dried uncooked apricots and peaches are high in iron.

Children and adults with weight problems should confine their fruit intake to three servings of fruit a day, and should stay away from the fruits that are high in calories. All food contains calories, but too many calories are fattening.

Helpful Hints to Heads of Households

Feature the deliciously nutritious!

Helpful Hints to Teachers

Have each student make a bumper sticker that says: Eat the deliciously nutritious! "Take homes" help the rest of the family, too.

CHAPTER NINE:

Raw Vegetables, Vegetable Drinks, Vegetable Concoctions

Together, raw vegetables and fruits provide *vitamins,* particularly vitamin A (important for vision, also keeps skin and membranes infection resistent) and vitamin C (makes healthy collagen, the glue that holds body cells together; permits healing; promotes resistance to infection; and keeps blood vessels sound) and *natural sugars and starches.* These natural carbohydrates provide all the energy anyone needs, unless a doctor says otherwise in a specific case. People do not need heaping spoonfuls of sugar on everything and sugary or starchy junk foods to get sugar. Quick energy from an apple makes more nutritional sense than quick energy from a candy bar because of the latter's cumulative bad side effects.

Invisible Vegetables Are As Valuable As Those Children See: Stowaways

Children should be offered three (half-cup) servings of fruit or juice a day and lots of vegetables or vegetable juices. As much vegetable as we can get them to eat (without creating anxiety or pressure) is good for them —certainly one yellow and one green vegetable each day. These can be served directly or indirectly as ingredients in other dishes or juices. It's no more nutritious to confront a vegetable head on when eating it than to eat it unwittingly as an invisible ingredient. Many a child has developed dislike for vegetables, *not* because of their taste, but because of the *issue* eating them represents. One great thing vegetables do for us, in addition to their famous vitamin contribution, is make us feel full, thus helping us avoid excessive snacking. Vegetables provide fiber. Fiber is good for the digestive system.

Vegetables, in small but worthwhile amounts, can be added to other foods as stowaways. For example, a little shredded parsley and grated carrot can be mixed in with the hamburger meat or meat loaf; a small amount of puréed mixed deep yellow and deep green vegetables can be stirred in the stew gravy or soup broth, etc.

Expect Children to Eat Vegetables

Children aren't necessarily enemies of vegetables. Contrary to popular opinion, children eat plenty of vegetables, if:

- The home or school lunch is full of attractively and tastily prepared varieties of vegetable snacks (and no competing junk foods).
- These vegetables appear as part of meals with the expectation that they will be chosen and some small amount (at least) of one or another (not necessarily all those served) will be eaten.
- Children can choose
  —*which* vegetables,
  —*when* to eat them,
  —*how much* to eat,
  —*raw or cooked,*
  —*with or without sauce,* and
  —at the *meal* or as *snacks.*
- Eating vegetables is not promoted as a Victorian issue of virtue, but rather as a routinely enjoyable activity, just as is eating cookies.

Grownups can make the decision that some vegetables will be eaten each day. If children have opportunities to make many decisions about eating vegetables, it's fair for grownups to make some decisions too.

Boiled Vegetables

Scientists say that raw vegetables do have slightly more nutrients, but not many more nutrients, than currectly cooked fresh or frozen vegtables. Correctly cooked—from a nutritional point of view—means *briefly* cooked, in a very small amount of rapidly *boiling* water, with a *lid* on, so vitamins don't steam away. A waterless cooker, pressure cooker, or double boiler is a good idea since only a few spoonfuls of water need to be used to cook vegetables in these utensils. The less cooking, the prettier the colors of cooked vegetables. The less cooking, the tastier flavor the vegetables will have. Many children who refuse vegetables have good reason; they've never had them expertly cooked.

Mother-myths aside, many of our nation's children *do* eat *small* servings of *slightly* boiled, *still colorful*, lightly "buttered" (with 100 percent corn oil margarine):

Fresh asparagus tips (or cold asparagus with vinegar and oil dressing).

Fresh broccoli flowers.

Fresh spinach (perhaps pureed with lemon in the blender).

Cabbage, white or red (but hardly cook it, only till pliable).

Beets (hot and buttery, or pickled and pretty).

Lima beans (but they become mealy if overcooked).

Turnips or rutabagas (mashed and buttered).

Artichoke leaves (the children enjoy dipping each leaf in melted margarine).

Fresh green peas (picking them from the pods is fun).

Fresh green beans.

Stewed tomatoes.

Barely boiled buttery baby onions sprinkled with green scallion.

Summer squash (or that kind of frozen squash that looks like mashed potatoes. Put it in a well-oiled baking dish and bake at 350 degrees for 30 minutes; meanwhile, sauté ¼ cup walnuts or pecans and a small amount of onion in corn oil; add cinnamon, nutmeg, and a little brown sugar; stir into squash).

Basics About Vegetables

A healthy, beautifully decorative and extremely delicious way to cook fresh vegetables is to slice, dice, or chop them; drop them into a pan, the bottom of which is covered with hot vegetable oil (Wesson, Mazola); sauté them over moderate heat stirring frequently, and eat (with or without 100 percent corn oil margarine [*not* butter]), or soy sauce, or other sauce. Boiling vegetables to death in the typical American manner significantly reduces the nourishment they contain. So does soaking. Somewhere, Adelle Davis wrote, "Surely the stoical eating of waterlogged, tastless boiled vegetables is proof that Americans have character." Schools take the prize for ruining vegetables; probably because they claim to aim at character building.

We can take our choice about vegetables. Many nutrients and much roughage lie in the peel. If we chop or thinly slice the vegetables, nobody will notice they still contain peel, anyway. But chemicals collect in the peel of root vegetables, so we may want to peel them. Authorities have strenuous and opposite advice on this point. But no authority says we should omit vegetables or that they're bad for the health, and most authorities say we should eat *more* vegetables. Frozen vegetables lose nutrients while thawing, so are best for us when put frozen into a small amount of boiling water. With all vegetables, brief, lidded, cooking is best.

Broiled Vegetables and Vegetable Juices

Broiling vegetables brushed with oil makes vegetables children often ask for more of. Vegetable juices can be very nourishing, tasty, and provide nice variety, but it isn't necessary for children to drink them since relatively the same nourishment can be obtained from raw or briefly cooked vegetables. Also, vegetable juices lack the bulk and fiber many Americans so desperately need. Two other vitrues of the humble vegetable are that it does *not* carry the (1) calorie and (2) cholesterol problems that worry many people. Potatoes and avocados are exceptions, but both are excellent foods anyway.

Raw Vegetable Ideas

Raw vegetables such as cauliflower, carrots, cucumber rounds with peel, cabbage and red cabbage curls, green beans, broccoli flowers, brussel sprouts on toothpicks, piles of peas and green pepper rings served with lemon juice, with salad dressing to dip in, or a standard dip, are usually a delight to young children. Serve these vegetables singly, in a colorful arrangement on a platter, in a tumbled mixture, or skewered on toothpicks. Children love to make vegetable designs and arrangements and, while engrossed in their art work, will probably consume a healthy assortment. And would you believe? Some children like parsley dunked in French dressing.

Speaking of dips and dressings, many children and teenagers who won't touch salad will eat the *parts* of it if these are served *separately* as vegetables and dips. Try these dips:

• Half catsup, half mayonnaise
• Dill pickle juice
• Vinegar, oil, salt and pepper as usual, then lots of curry, lemon, sugar, tarragon, oregano, basil, pap-

rika, corriander, rosemary, celery salt, powdered
boullion, and so on. Kids will like it better if they
help make it.

A bowl of thawed but uncooked, crystal-filled, colorful frozen mixed vegetables goes over in a big way with
many children. Don't introduce the idea of salting these
vegetables, but if it's salted vegetables or *no* vegetables,
sprinkle on a little liveliness. Never set out the salt
shaker though, there'll be no end to it then.*

Surprise baggies: Fill transparent sandwich baggies
with assorted raw vegetables and fasten with a twister.
Fine when friends come to play. Easy for teens to take
wherever they're going.

Vegetable sandwiches: Whole-grain bread with lettuce,
tomato, and mayonnaise; cucumbers, parsley and mayonnaise; peanut butter and carrot shavings; any of the
vegetable spreads in *Recipes for a Small Planet.* (As
many mothers know, quite a few children care more
about the mayonnaise than the official sandwich filling
anyway, so if we call it a mayonnaise sandwich, we can
get away with including the vegetables.) Another idea:
Salad-loving children like salad sandwiches. Children
who are keen on mustard or catsup will eat vegetable
sandwiches camouflaged with these favorites:

Avocado boats: Avocados are marvelously rich in nutrients of many kinds. They are also filling. Many children love to eat an avocado boat (half an avocado)
filled with a pool of salad dressing.† Avocados are
magnificently nutritious.

Here are three "vegetable sandwiches" many children
like. Sometimes children eat vegetables when they (and
we) don't notice:

* Yes, salt. Nutritionists aren't against salt, used moderately.
The idea is to avoid heavily salted snack foods, and sitting at
the table trying to make each type of food on the plate think
our sprinkle-happy salt shakers are snow-making machines.

† Avocados are high in calories. Calorie watchers should
avoid avocados.

Steak sandwich Put minute steak, lettuce, tomato, cooked onion, mayonnaise and mustard on a whole wheat *bun*.

Chicken sandwich: put crunchy spinach leaves and carrot shavings dipped in lemon and oil between the slice of chicken and the dark bread, then spread with mayonnaise.

Tuna sandwich: With chopped celery, onion, and green pepper, plus old faithful, mayonnaise.

Most children will also be tempted when they see a platter of celery or cooked and hollowed brussel sprouts stuffed with:

• peanut butter
• cottage cheese (with or without carroway seeds),
• cream cheese (with or without diced green peppers), or
• cheese (not cheese spreads, which are easier to stuff in, but are less "good" food).

Even two-year-olds can help stuff the celery or brussel sprouts. Helping makes the eating more special. Celery is an excellent source of fiber, and many children enjoy it. Brussel sprouts are a relative of cabbage and are very nourishing.

Any of the above, ready and waiting after naptime, usually go fast. Teenagers generally will eat anything nibbly if it's set in front of them and if nothing else is easily accessible. If teens complain about the absence of soft drinks and potato chips in the home, parents can say, "We're trying to make it harder for all of us to eat the wrong food. That is, we're trying to make it easier to eat right. You can buy junk food elsewhere if you absolutely have to, but we don't want to tease and tempt ourselves and _____ (any younger children)." Raw vegetables can go to school in baggies. Glaze-eyed TV gazers will unthinkingly snack on vegetables rather than on less desirable foods if presented with them. And even the housewife or househusband

who hates to cook can't legitimately claim that it's too
tedious to slice and peel a heap of raw vegetables or
to pour a packet of frozen vegetables into a pretty dish.
When it comes to carrots, folks may want to note that
carrots release the vitamin A they contain much better
if cooked briefly, but many children prefer raw carrots.
If raw carrots will be eaten and cooked carrots will be
spurned, then common sense tells us that raw carrots
will be more nourishing than no carrots.

Vegetable Soups and Spreads

Vegetable soups abound in the cookbooks recommended at the end of this book. Soups are nice in
lunchbox soup containers, as after-school snacks, for
lunch, as a dinner starter, or as a bedtime snack. For
example, have you tried cream of celery, pea, or bean
soup (made with skim milk or water and a few spoons
of bran as thickener), lentil soup, black bean soup,
beet soup, potato soup, onion soup, or gazpacho? All
soups need herbs and seasonings.

Many soups not *labeled* vegetable soups have lots of
vegetables in them. For example, beef and barley soup
usually includes parsley, celery, onion, carrots, peas,
tomato, and so on. Any soup can go to school in a
thermos. Homemade soups are spectacular and take
only 20 to 30 minutes to make (and can be made of
leftovers while washing dishes or doing other kitchen
duties). Canned soups containing vegetables can be
"vegetable-enriched" with a few quickly cut and briefly
boiled additions to help serve the purpose: providing
the people we feed with more vegetables. Many children who allegedly don't eat vegetables eat vegetables
in soups.

Here are a few favorite homemade soups:

Mushroom soup: Sauté mushrooms in corn oil. With
them, sauté parsley, onion and celery. Melt 100 percent
corn oil margarine. Stir in whole wheat flour and a can
of creamed chicken soup. Put together and add nutmeg, chives, paprika. Serve hot.

Cabbage soup: Cook 4 lbs. shredded cabbage and 2 chopped onions in butter for 15 minutes. Sprinkle with 2 tablespoons whole wheat flour and add 4 cups water, stirring till boils. Add 2 cups canned tomatoes, salt, pepper, 2 tablespoons sugar, 2 tablespoons lemon juice, carraway seeds. Cook 1 hour and serve hot with sour cream. (Sour cream is high in calories and cholesterol, but if we usually watch out for both, here's a chance for a treat.)

Beet soup: Peel and chop: ½ cup carrots, 1 cup onions, 2 cups beets. Boil gently for 20 minutes. Add, and boil 15 minutes more: 1 tablespoon lemon juice, 1 tablespoon 100 percent corn oil margarine, 2 cups canned boullion soup, 1 cup shredded cabbage. Serve hot or cold with boiled new potatoes, hard boiled egg halves and sour cream.

Tomato soup: Put 10 whole tomatoes in deep pot with corn oil covering bottom. Cut up in pot when soft enough. Add salt, pepper and garlic powder. Reduce heat, cover, and simmer for 1 hour. Add 1 onion, finely chopped. Cook for ½ hour more, and serve hot or cold.

Chilled Gazpacho: Peel, cut and prepare these vegetables and purée them in blender: 1 onion, 1 cucumber, 1 green pepper (without seeds), 3 tomatoes. Add ¼ cup wine vinegar, ¼ cup olive oil, 1 cup canned tomato juice, salt, a touch of tabasco sauce, and tarragon. Serve cold with minced cucumber, onion, and green pepper floating on top.

Remember, a little goes a long way when it comes to nutrients. For a small person, a few sips of vegetable soup respresent a lot of vitamins. However, most *young* children prefer *canned* soup, so the objective becomes "souping up the soup," by putting in extra vegetables.

Blender-made fresh herbed and seasoned vegetable spreads on (whole grain) crackers are delicious. Once or twice a week, children enjoy helping to make them and to eat them, if they are treated as a treat. The spread can be put in a separate container in a lunch box and spread on the crackers with a plastic knife at lunch time so sogginess doesn't set in.

Example number 1: Tomato spread: 1 cup blended tomatoes (purée), ¼ cup grated cheese, ¼ cup soy grits. Sesame seeds and herbs to taste. (If soy grits sound too much like health fad food to you, think of another nutritious thickener.)

Example number 2: Carrot-nut spread: 1 cup pecans, 1 cup cut carrots, 1 tablespoon of vegetable oil, squeeze of lemon, dill. (There are many more in the cookbooks suggested.)

Example number 3: Ava-tacos: Mash or blenderize an avocado, add lemon juice, chill powder, garlic & onion salt and put in taco shells. (They can be purchased in supermarkets).

Vegetable Juices

Example number 1: Combination juice
½ can sauerkraut
½ can tomato

Example number 2: Canned juice, such as V-8 juice

(For the noncook, there are all sorts of canned vegetable juices in supermarkets. We can mix, match, and add our own odd perker-upper seasonings.)

Or use a juicer. As a "special" event, the child can choose exotic combinations of vegetables and herbs for her juice once or twice a week. Parents frequently are presented with a choice between convention and nutrition. For instance, a little boy who "never" ate vegetables, one breakfast asked over and over if he could "squoosh" tomatoes and make juice. The paternal answer? "We don't eat tomatoes for breakfast!"

Salads

Not always the same old kinds, but interesting salads and dressings such as those in the recommended cookbooks, can be served as the main dish at lunch and *first* at dinner. This helps fill people up before they finish the main dishes, still feeling hungry for dessert. Some children love salads, and *all* children can be expected to eat a big bite or more. In the case of a small person, there's relatively quite a bit of nutrition in a bite.

We can cut *small* amounts of unfamiliar but top-notch vitamin A-filled, dark leafy green vegetables into salads: beet tops, broccoli flowers or leaves, Chinese cabbage and Chinese celery, kale, parsley, Swiss chard, turnip tops, watercress. Did you know? The deeper the green, the more nutrients the vegetable contains? Thus broccoli, spinach, parsley, and watercress are more nourishing than lettuce.

If children don't like salads, it may be because those they've been expected to eat were watery, wilted, and weary. First, make sure greens are dry, not watery. After washing them, pat them dry with a dish towel. Second, make sure greens are fresh and cold, not wilted. Third, make salad last and add dressing as you sit down at the table so the leaves won't go limp. Some samples of salads we've seen children enjoy follow, but there are many more in the cookbooks listed at the end of this book:

Cabbage and green pepper salad: Chop crunchy green peppers and red cabbage and top with any favorite dressing. Water chestnuts add yet *more* crunch.

Fresh spinach salad: Spinach leaves without stems and a dressing that's half mustard, half olive oil, seasoned with lemon juice, pepper and garlic.

Celery cabbage (also called Chinese cabbage): Cut in skinny slivers, with vinegar and oil dressing.

Orange salad: Canned mandarin oranges or fresh orange sections can be used; mix them with onion slices so thin that the rings fall apart and crisp spinach leaves; any dressing, and add black olives, raisins, or chopped nuts, if children like them.

Puerto Vallarta watercress salad: To watercress, add pine nuts, drained bacon bits and nicely sliced mushrooms.

Grapefruit and avocado salad: Half and half, chilled, with a lemon and olive oil dressing.

Broccoli and mixed vegetables: Pour a dressing of: 1 egg yolk, 1 teaspoon mustard, 2 tablespoons vinegar, 6 tablespoons olive oil, salt and pepper, over cut up broccoli, carrots, red cabbage, radishes and scallion greens.

Any greens and any raw vegetables, especially colorful ones, can go into salad. Tomatoes and radishes are red, but remember other bright ideas too. Bean sprouts, bamboo shoots and water chestnuts are dull looking, but add texture; all are crunchy. And you may like the funky taste of mushrooms. Quite a few children like salad for breakfast.

Two cold vegetables that aren't exactly salads, but that stand in their stead:

* Soak sliced cucumbers and sliced onions in salt water for 15 minutes until soft, rinse, add salt, pepper, sugar, vinegar, and mayonnaise.

* Freeze canned tomatoes and chopped scallions in an ice tray; serve cold with curried mayonnaise.

Vegetable Main Dishes: Most of These Vegetable Possibilities Can Also Go to School in a Lunch Box

Serve vegetables frequently as an optional side dish part of dinner. This enables children to get used to these foods gradually. They will soon stop regarding them as "weird." Consider: children and mates can choose a new dish or the raw vegetable platter, or the juice, or the salad, if an *assortment* of vegetables is served. As we learn to cook these "peculiar" dishes comfortably, and as children become friendly with them, they can become main dishes. (See recommended cookbooks for exciting new ideas: such things as vegetable pancakes, loaves, puddings, rings, stews, casseroles with herbs and sauces; Chinese-style vegetable-loaded dishes; tomatoes or peppers stuffed with delicious fillings; and vegetable stuffings for whole roast chickens.) A cherished myth of the cook who dislikes cooking is that all such dishes are time-consuming, hard to make, and require a "stove-slave" to produce. On the contrary, quick and easy recipes are readily available. They also bring a fringe benefit: no greasy meat pans to scour.

Some Vegetable Main Dishes and Major Side Dishes

Children may not like these, but fathers and mothers might. Sometimes children *later* learn to like foods familiar from their childhoods. See what happens if you serve these as *side dishes* at first:

Swiss eggplant: Peel an eggplant and dice coarsely; sauté in corn oil with chopped onion; add cut up tomatoes; now bake at 350 degrees for half an hour, with swiss cheese on top of the last 15 minutes.

Crusted cauliflower casserole: Prepare ¼ cup brown rice as usual; meanwhile, purée 3 cups briefly steamed cauliflower and ½ cup chicken broth (comes in a can) in the blender; stir in ½ cup finely chopped cheddar-type cheese, ½ cup chopped roasted peanuts, ¼ cup whole wheat flour, ½ cup wheat germ, and nutmeg. Mix cooked brown rice and cauliflower mixture; pour into oiled baking dish, cover with cheddar cheese and more nutmeg. Bake at 350 degrees, for 25 minutes.

Broiled, stuffed tomatoes: Preheat oven to 400 degrees; cut tomatoes in half across (take the top off); spread on a mix of mustard, garlic, scallions, basil, parsley, thyme, olive oil, wheat germ; broil for 15 minutes; pour sautéed onion, mushroom and chicken in and over tomatoes.

Killed cabbage: Sauté till tasty ½ cup chopped onion, ½ cup wheat germ, 1 cup tomato, and 6 cups chopped cabbage in vegetable oil; add ¼ cup chopped ham, 2 tablespoons bacon drippings, garlic, 1 tablespoon vinegar, pepper and a little water.

(See section on legumés, nuts and seeds for lots more recipes containing vegetables.)

Vegetable Sauces

Vegetable sauces are simple to make, make vegetables fancier, and are often a clever way to get valuable nutrients into children. For example:

Put two just-out-of-the refrigerator egg yolks, the juice of 2 lemons, and some 100 percent corn-oil margarine into a room-temperature pot, put the pot on a low burner, stir until margarine has melted (two minutes) and you have luscious Hollandaise sauce.

Here's a good sauce: Melt butter or 100 percent corn-oil margarine, add minced onion, lemon juice, and pepper.

For brown sauce: sauté diced carrot, onion, and celery in corn oil, sprinkle with whole wheat flour, add canned beef bouillon, some tomato paste, bay leaf, and thyme. When cooked, liquify in blender. Delicious over many vegetables.

Or make cream sauce: Let margarine melt over a low flame, add milk powder and whole wheat flour, stir till it thickens, and you have an instant sauce containing milk and whole grain. (Add Worchestershire, bits of cheese, carraway, onion, nutmeg, pepper, mushrooms, etc. to taste.)

Tomato sauce is delicious on vegetables: Many children are spaghetti-sauce freaks. Thus, pouring ready-made or your own made-in-bulk-and-frozen spaghetti sauce over any vegetable makes many vegetables attractive to them. Prepared pizza sauce on vegetables is popular, too. In vegetable oil, sauté chopped onion, chopped celery, chopped carrot, add a can of tomatoes, a spoonful of dark molasses, pepper, etc., to taste.

Or just drop crumbley bouillon in the few spoons of water in which the vegetable is boiled.

Mustard sauce: Blend strong mustard with melted 100 percent corn-oil margarine.

Dill butter: Put dill, lemon juice, and 100 percent corn-oil margarine in blender.

Parsley butter: Blenderize margarine, chopped parsley, lots of lemon juice and cayenne pepper.

Vinaigrette Sauce: Stir together *⅝ corn oil, ⅜ vinegar; garlic, pepper, capers, onion, parsley, chives, tarragon, chervil, egg yolk, yogurt, lemon juice and dill.*

Wheat germ in melted margarine is marvelous on almost any cooked vegetable.

More Popular Vegetable Suggestions

Vegetable jackpot is fun—toss an assortment of colorful vegetables slightly sautéed in vegetable oil, into a casserole or cooked brown rice—mix—and see what "finds" children can make.

Classrooms with cooking corners or curriculums can involve kids in projects like those below, as well as in making more conventional dishes. Many children enjoy the following "home or school" vegetables:

A slice of acorn squash, baked with margarine, molasses (both added at the end);

Asparagus (*tips* only) or broccoli (flowers only) with Hollandaise (many children dislike the stalk);

Cauliflower flowers with hot cheese or tomato sauce;

Round slices of *slightly* boiled yellow squash with tomato sauce;

A platter of sliced carrots and sliced apples brushed with lemon juice and vegetable oil, topped with wheat germ (like bread crumbs and very nourishing), and baked briefly on a cookie sheet; or

Chilled string beans with salad dressing.

There are many other vegetable treats to offer the people you feed.

Children who like grilled cheese will often eat a vegetable baked with a slice of cheese on top of it—summer squash rounds, a cored tomato, or a cored green pepper.

Vegetable patties are popular: chop any vegetable (potato, cabbage, carrot) or a mixture of them in a blender, mix with egg to glue the mixture together, add seasoning to taste, form patties, roll in wheat germ and sauté in vegetable oil. This is a terrific way to take advantage of leftovers.

Most children like potatoes, which are full of vitamin C and iron. Potatoes shouldn't be soaked, scrubbed ferociously, set aside to sit after peeling, cooked twice, or cooked long. The rules of retaining nutrients in other vegetables apply to potatoes too.

Most children also like corn: corn on the cob boiled briefly or roasted; cooked frozen corn-*off*-the-cob; corn in cream sauce; corn patties with egg, and wheat germ, slightly sautéed in vegetable oil, corn pudding, etc.

Children enjoy making Japanese "tempura" vegetables: Take any two vegetables and make into small interesting shapes (broccoli or cauliflower flowers, squash rounds, carrot sticks, eggplant cubes, etc.). Dip into a very thick batter of whole wheat flour, beaten eggs, soy sauce, and water, and drop into 3″ of *hot,* hot vegetable oil: drain on a paper towel. Incidentally, this is a great way to introduce new vegetables, which can later be presented in a more recognizable form.

None of these vegetable ideas, with the exception of certain of the casseroles, loaves, etc., take more than 20 minutes to prepare. The troublesome dishes given in cookbooks like *Recipes for a Small Planet* can be skipped, used for special occasions, *or modified to be made more practical yet equally as delicious.*

Slim As a Bean Sprout Svelte as a Bamboo Shoot

Have you discovered lowcal, crispy, crunchy bean sprouts, bamboo shoots, and water chestnuts, available in cans at most supermarkets? They add a welcome texture contrast to stews, soups, salads, and casseroles, and are delicious in dip or as adornment for a roast.

Vegetable Motivation

The more it's possible to involve preschool and elementary school age children in growing vegetables (providing it isn't real farm-style child labor, which generally causes children to migrate to the city as soon as they're of age and become vegetable haters as well), the more it's generally possible to get them to *eat* vegetables. Books such as *Creative Food Experiences for Children* (see end of book) are full of ideas and information about vegetables: categories, science experiments, fun facts, children's books to accompany vegetable projects, and recipes. Varieties of interesting activities with vegetables will increase motivation during vegetable month and throughout the ten-month conversion project. They can help develop a healthy, lifetime way of eating.

Teenagers are quite interested in themselves. Self-focused activities at home and school tend to go over better than other kinds of studies. Teens are also developing skills in making sensible judgments about their own lives. *If left alone with this food conversion project, and not interfered with by parents,* they are likely to go as far with it as any group. Unless you know that your men and women are destined to become home economics majors, you who teach a wide variety of subjects, including Sunday school, may want to work food projects into your programs. Otherwise, the teens won't learn nutrition.

Vegetable and Vitamin Information, or Alternatives to Spinach

Some vegetables are more important than others. For instance, no one ever suffered from malnutrition because he passed up eggplant, peppers, or cucumbers. It isn't necessary for a child to eat *all kinds* of vegetables to get *all kinds* of vitamins. Those folks not interested in detailed vitamin data can skip the following paragraphs, and remember just one general principle: serve a wide variety of vegetables in a wide variety of forms, and all necessary vitamins will be offered. In fact, they may even be *eaten.* For other folks . . .

Vitamin A

If he eats *one* of the following every day or every few days, a child will get enough *vitamin A* for normal growth, good eyesight, and good skin, resistance to sores, etc.:

1. A dark yellow vegetable (carrots, winter squash, sweet potatoes) * *or*
2. A dark leafy vegetable (broccoli, spinach, kale, parsley, collards, cabbage—lettuce isn't dark green

---

* Corn isn't classified as a deep yellow vegetable, and it is not a good source of vitamin A, though it's fine for fiber.

and isn't particularly full of vitamin A, but it does provide needed bulk).

3. If he hates all of the above, there's good vitamin A in apricots, peaches, cantaloupe, and pumpkins.
4. If he eats none of these either, liver is loaded with vitamin A, and there's some in eggs, whole milk, cheese, and margarine or butter. V-8 juice contains vitamin A. Some people who ordinarily dislike liver have been found to love it, once they've tasted it broiled and smothered in onions, green olive slices, and bacon. Remember, though, that bacon is full of dangerous nitrites. Nitrite-free bacon can be purchased in some parts of the country. If bacon is served only *rarely,* and only as an *ingredient,* most nutritionists would probably not complain.

Vitamin B

Except for dark leafy green vegetables, there are better sources of B vitamins than vegetables. The child can get all the B vitamins she needs from lean meat, fish, poultry, eggs, milk, peanuts, peanut butter, and whole grains. If she'll eat beans, peas, and salads, that's perfect.

Vitamin C

Raw cabbage (children will usually eat it with dip—catsup and mayonnaise is a favorite—or in the form of cole slaw); brussel sprouts (good with lemon butter); green peppers (raw or stuffed and cooked—don't swallow your gum in surprise, but there *are* children who eat whole green crunchy peppers like apples); broccoli (many children love the "blossom" part of it with lemon butter); tomatoes (juice, wedges, slices with mayonnaise, in a sandwich, stuffed or stewed); potatoes with peel; mustard and turnip greens, and collards all contain vitamin C. People can get their C even if they eat *no* vegetables, providing they eat the several fruits which are excellent sources. These are oranges,

grapefruits, other citrus fruits, cantaloupes, and strawberries. At one convenient time or another, we can try
them all and settle for serving those which family members (including each child and adult) do like. Most
children like potatoes, which, if cooked right, contain
vitamin C.

Vitamin D and E

It isn't necessary to eat vegetables for the sake of
vitamin D (because it isn't in vegetables) or for the
sake of E, which is better available elsewhere, although
it can be gotten by eating leafy vegetables and legumes.

Vitamin K

Leafy vegetables are a good source of K. If children
won't eat salads, they can get K from cauliflower, liver,
and eggs. Many children like raw cauliflower dipped in
half mayonnaise, half catsup. Eggs, raw or cooked, can
easily be smuggled into beverages, sauces, or dishes of
many kinds.

Minerals

All of the minerals needed by the body (calcium,
iron, phosphorus, magnesium, iodine, flouride, sodium,
potassium, and trace minerals) can be obtained from
foods other than vegetables, though certain dark leafy
vegetables—collards, kale, mustard greens, turnip
greens, and lima beans—contain some minerals, and
are especially high in iron. However, the body doesn't
absorb iron from vegetables as well as it absorbs it
from meat.

Why Promote Vegetables?

Probably the four most important reasons for encouraging children and other people to enjoy vegetables
are:

- Providing a wide variety of pretty, tasty vegetables allows parents and other adults to be *generous,* to be *givers of food,* and to be *givers of love* (people have universally felt food to be a symbol of love). We can be all of these while we are starting to remove and withhold excess amounts of sugary foods, salty foods, foods with coloring, flavoring—including sweeteners like saccharin—nitrates/nitrites, and white flour. It's wise indeed to have some new treats and surprises to add to our tables and shelves while we withdraw other offerings and allowables, or we'll find ourselves perceived by our children as worse than witches and ogres.

- Hard, raw vegetables are nature's toothbrush. Animals that eat vegetables have no dentists or toothbrushes, but they have healthy teeth. Eating fresh vegetables is an especially useful form of dental care for the *young* child who usually isn't a very reliable or skillful toothbrusher, if he bothers to brush at all. Teenagers are more likely to care about their teeth for cosmetic and social reasons. If adults key into it, this concern about good looking teeth, may cause teens to eat more raw vegetables.

- Most vegetables, especially the unsugared vegetables such as broccoli, are excellent low-calorie, high-bulk fillers. Throughout life, we can munch all we like, thus satisfying "mouth hunger." We can eat to be sociable. We can avoid hunger without getting fat. Eating more watercress, spinach, cabbage, celery, lettuce, cucumber, peppers, bean sprouts, asparagus, broccoli, cauliflower, Chinese cabbage, mushrooms, parsley, summer squash, and French-style green beans is a good way to want less cake.

- Vegetables provide fiber, badly needed by most Americans to help them avoid heartburn, hemorrhoids, constipation, and obesity. We also need fiber to *attempt* to protect against cancer of the colon and rectum (which 99,000 people get each year and from which 49,000 die annually), ischemic heart disease—the prime cause of heart attacks (heart attacks kill 700,000 people per year), diverticular disease of the colon, appendicitis, phlebitis, and resulting blood clots to the lungs. However, vegetables aren't as good as whole grains in providing fiber, so people don't have to love celery—or other vegetables—if they eat lots of whole grains (see chapter on grains). And it's unlikely that as much protection against killers such as cancer and heart attack can be found in roughage of *any* kind, in *any* amount, as roughage proponents sincerely believe. Yet authorities generally think it advisable for Americans to eat more vegetables than they do.

What Can Teachers Do About Fruits and Vegetables?

This depends a great deal upon your situation. If you are an *early* childhood education person (with children 0-4 years of age) you can fairly well eliminate the no-no's from your classroom through motivating discussions at parent meetings, and the distribution to families of "good food idea sheets." Then you can develop your good food projects curriculum: using snack time, any meals your program serves, and your classroom cooking center as the core, and field trips, film strips, and so forth, as feasible. There are many children's picture books featuring food. If you use half the ideas in *Creative Food Experiences for Children* (see the bibliography at the end of this book) you'll have a fantastic nutrition education program.

If your children are five through twelve years of age, your children have some learnings to unlearn and habits to break. After piquing an interest with a vegetable farm or orchard field trip, or a short colorful film such as "Jenny Is a Good Thing," designate one day of the week as fruit and vegetable day. Homework for this day is always fruit or vegetable related. Some homework assignments might be:

• During the week, go to the store and count and list the *fresh* vegetables.

- Do the same with *frozen* vegetables another week.
- And *canned* vegetables yet *another* week.
- Repeat with fruits.
  (See related *classroom* project below.)
- Bring all the *green* vegetables you can find to school.
- Repeat with *yellow* vegetables.
- Bring in a fruit *sauce,* like applesauce.
- Bring in a dried fruit.
- Bring in a fruit that's orange, red or purple.
- Bring in a fruit that's yellow, gold or green.
- Bring in a white fruit.
  (And have a tasting party once a week.)
- Bring beautiful or tempting bowls, dishes, glasses and garnishes.
- On fruit and vegetable day, encourage children to include fruits and vegetables in their lunches.
- Ask parents for a favorite fruit or vegetable recipe. This may be salad, cooked, dessert, whatever. Children old enough to write should write the recipe; hopefully parents will write it for nonwriters.
  (See related classroom project below.)
- Write down every fruit or vegetable you eat this week. Do it daily so you don't forget. Bring the list in on fruit and vegetable day. Discuss, praising where appropriate, but never scolding.
- Read labels on artificial fruit-flavored drinks and discuss later in class.
- From time to time, have children bring raw vegetables for a buffet.
- For as many weeks as it takes, for a homework activity, give each child a duplicated information sheet about *one* vitamin or mineral (as presented in the vegetable chapter of this book). Ask the child to notice if she or her eats anything with that vitamin in it, and if not, please to do so. Tell the class what was eaten.
- Make posters for school hallways and for other classrooms showing why it's valuable to eat vegetables.
- Invent "knock-knock" jokes using the names of

fruits and vegetables. Make a joke book. This is usually a very popular project!

- Plan a lunch trip to a Chinese or vegetarian restaurant and eat delectable vegetable dishes.
- After children have brought in a family favorite fruit or vegetable recipe, have the recipes duplicated, and let each child make and decorate a "cookbook." This would make a nice present for parents.
- Have a fruit and vegetable bulletin board. Choose one child a week to be in charge of it. He or she can collect pictures, slogans, and so on all week (at home and from classmates) and can redecorate the board on fruit and vegetable day. Nutrition news clippings from newspapers and magazines can be included. There certainly are lots of them!
- On and off throughout the year, have children bring needed ingredients for raw vegetable platters and dips, and set out a serve-yourself buffet.
- Develop a salad bar, where salad is served with lunch once a week. Children can bring all the ingredients.
- After children have listed vegetables and fruits available to them as suggested above, have them make personal posters listing *only* vegetables and fruits the individual *likes*. Those disliked may not be mentioned. Have children decorate the posters with brilliant psychodelic poster paints and clip them *all* up on clotheslines criss-crossing the classroom.
- Make, mix, and drink fruit juices.
- Make vegetable soup in the classroom.
- Make fruit spread or fruit butter (who can bring the blender? Who can bring each needed ingredient? Who can eat the results?).
- Make and eat vegetable spreads on whole grain crackers.
- Make a fruit aspic using gelatin, not jello—discuss the difference.
- Make various dressings and sauces to serve with fruit.
- For the next class party, make a delectable compote

or cooked fruit concoction or fruit ice or sherbet—
let the children choose which.

If the children you teach are over twelve, it's likely
you only have them for one period a day. And perhaps
your subject is quite unrelated. However, if you think
nutrition education is important, you can fit it in, start
an extracurricular club, interest appropriate teachers in
leading these projects, or do something else. He who
cares, acts.

CHAPTER TEN:

Meat Meals with Less Meat

For breakfast, lunch, and dinner, meat-*less* meals (not necessarily entirely *meat*-less) can often be offered. Authorities agree that most Americans eat too much meat. Vegetarians say we should eat no meat. Scientists say eat less meat, but everyone agrees that people don't *need* meat more than a few times a week. In fact, it's hard to prove people need any meat to be fully nourished.

The meat we eat far breakfast is usually a pork product, with ham, sausage, and bacon the most traditional. We can serve these things less and less frequently without suddenly dropping them. As we decrease pork products and meat in general for breakfast, it's important that we *increase* other interesting foods. Many dinner dishes consist of or include meat, but don't demand having a thick slab of meat occupying a third of the plate, wedged between a scoop of mashed potato and a pile of peas.

Very healthful meals can be prepared without meat or with meat as just one part of a dish, such as a casserole. Even lunches, to take to school or work, can be packed without meat.

Lunchbags, -Boxes, -Buckets vs. the Fast-Food Industry

Anything that can be eaten for dinner makes a good lunchbox lunch of leftovers for mothers, fathers, teens, tens, and tots. Actually, anything that can be eaten for dinner or lunch can make an excellent breakfast as well.

Let's take a brief tangent to make the observation that *taking* lunch from home, and packing the children's lunches for them, is very likely the only way to be sure to have a clear idea of individual family members' complete daily diets. Few feeders of families actually *know* what their families eat during the day. Meal planners think in terms of the one, two, or three meals *they* provide each day, not realizing that they probably *provide* less than half of what any person involved *eats*. Maids and mothers are fast being replaced as major providers of their families' food, not by fathers, but by mass-produced, mass-marketed, pseudo-food manufacturers and their fast food service colleagues.

If we care what our kids eat, we're better off helping them fix super good lunches—so good that classmates will envy them—then trusting to the junk food pushers to attend to children's nutritional well-being.

But instead of those old nitrite-ridden standbys such as ham and bologna, how about other kinds of meat and nonmeat sandwich fillings, or thermos cannisters containing meat-*less* meat dishes such as:

Stews and Similar Dishes

Rosemary stew with dumplings: Coat bite size bits of lean beef with whole-wheat flour and pepper; brown slowly in corn oil; add lots of chopped onion and cook till onion is transparent; stir in 2 cups boiling water in which 2 bouillon cubes have been dissolved. Add a bay leaf, 1 teaspoon thyme, 1 teaspoon rosemary. Cover and cook slowly for an hour and a half. Add 1 cup cut carrots and 1 cup cut celery, and cook till vegetables are tender. Add a tablespoon of bran for fiber. Separately, combine 1½ teaspoons baking powder with 1½ cups whole-wheat flour, stir in chopped parsley and a handful of bran in another container, combine 2 beaten eggs, 2 tablespoons melted 100 percent corn oil margarine, ⅜ cup skim milk. Put the two mixtures together and spread on top of stew. Cover, let dough steam till it looks tasty. Serve with tossed green salad for dinner. Or, put in a thermos and include in a lunchbox.

Braised beef and vegetables: Cube inexpensive beef without fat, roll in whole-wheat flour and pepper. Sauté slowly in medium-temperature corn oil. Place in casserole with 2 cups boiling water; cover tightly and bake at 250 degrees for an hour. Then add chopped carrots, onions, celery, potato, or other vegetables the family likes and bake for an additional half hour. At the end, add a can of beef gravy or make your own (see standard cookbook) and, if you like, add a sprinkling of uncooked frozen corn or peas for bright color.

Irish stew: Cube lamb, dredge it in whole-wheat flour seasoned with garlic, brown it in corn oil over a medium flame. Remove the meat, set aside and sauté onion slices in the pan. Put lamb back in, cover with boiling water, cover tightly, and simmer for 1½ hours. Separately, partially boil cubed potatoes, carrots and turnips; add to meat and onion mixture, simmer with lid on for 20 minutes. Blend 2 tablespoons of whole-wheat flour into melted 100 percent corn oil margarine and fold into the hot stew to thicken it.

Cookbooks abound with sumptuous stews. For another taste treat, try leftover stew (freeze it and bring it back a week later) poured over freshly prepared brown rice, dotted with scallion confetti, and with oven melted slices of yellow cheese on top. Stews can be made during evenings and weekends, and then can be whipped out after work for a quick supper. Perhaps once a week, one of the above, with fresh fruit, will provide welcome variety to the tiresome lunchbox sandwich.

Meat Soups*

Beef and barley soup: Brown one pound of lean hamburger in corn oil; put it and 8 cups of hot water in soup pot. When water boils, add ½ cup barley, and a soup bone if you have one. Cover and boil 45 minutes. Meanwhile, sauté in corn oil: fine sliced carrots, onion, celery, and tomatoes (or use a can of tomatoes) until vegetables are fairly tender. Then add salt, pepper, garlic powder and lots of chopped parsley. Add the beef and vegetables to the water and barley. Stir, cover, and let simmer for a few minutes. Add half a pack of frozen mixed vegetables for color, and serve five minutes later.†

Super "stoup" (stew-soup): Sauté lean hamburger, chopped potato, tomato, onion, carrots, and celery. When the mixture looks cooked, pour in 4 cups of hot water and add lots of chopped cabbage. Let mixture come to boil, and boil 10 minutes. Add a large can of prepared spaghetti, pizza, or manicotti sauce, 1 can beef gravy, garlic and pepper and stir. Serve with homemade biscuits or bread. (See GRAIN chapter for wholesome recipes.)

Gramma Max's chicken soup: Put in a pot pieces of a plump broiling chicken. Add chopped onion (1), carrot (2), celery (3), and 4 cups water. Bring to a boil and simmer, lidded, for 15 minutes. Add ½ cup rice. Lid, simmer for an hour-and-a-half. Remove chicken and serve separately.

Hot dog soup: This much hot dog and bacon probably won't hurt many people—prepare homemade, powdered, or canned thick pea soup; then add 2 tablespoons melted 100 percent corn oil margarine, and already sautéed celery, onion, carrots, and hot dog

---

* (As the main event for supper, or for a once-a-week-lunch box treat)

† To any of these soups, you can add a small amount of bran for valuable roughage.

slices. Sprinkle before serving with bacon bits and Parmesan cheese.

Ham soup: Boil a ham bone with lots of chunks of meat on it in 6 cups of water. As soon as water boils, add 1 cup barley, 3 fresh tomatoes cut up, plus carrots, celery, and pepper. Simmer 45 minutes. Cool, skim off fat; heat and serve.

Beef ball soup: Add baby lean beef balls previously sautéed in corn oil, tarragon, and chives or scallions, to hot canned or powdered beef noodle soup. With a special homemade baked treat and an extra good salad, you're all set for supper or have come up with a wow of a lunch.

Italian Style Low-Meat Favorites

Pizza: Buy it or bake it. To bake your own, heat oven to 425 degrees. Dissolve 1 package active dry yeast in water and add 2½ cups Bisquick,* 1 tablespoon bran, and beat. Knead 20 times on floured surface. Divide into 4 parts and roll into 4 paper-thin 10″ circles. Put on a well-oiled baking sheet and form a ½″ rim on each pizza. Spread with the following mixture and bake for 20 minutes: 2 cups tomato sauce, 2 tablespoons olive oil, ¾ chopped onion, garlic, pepper, oregano, lots of sliced mushrooms, and a layer of mozarella cheese. Or use the pizza sauce that comes in a jar.

Spaghetti with meat saure: Use your favorite ready-made sauce in a jar from the supermarket, or see any cookbook and make it once a month and freeze it. To make a delicious sauce yourself: slice onion into corn or olive oil, add ground beef, sliced mushrooms, chopped celery, and 1 tablespoon bran. Sauté over low flame. Add canned tomato sauce and tomato paste, garlic, salt, pepper. Serve over brown spaghetti, if pos-

---

* Yes, Bisquick, white flour, premade, preservatives and all. Remember? We believe in occasional exceptions, and in *improvement*: eating less meat is probably more important than *always* avoiding all white flour.

sible. If being overweight is a problem, serve this sauce over eggplant or spinach instead of spaghetti.

Oriental-Style Meals for Dinner and as Lunch the Next Day

Ginger beef and vegetables: Ask your butcher to cut flank steak into long skinny pieces or do it yourself, if you have a sharp knife and time. Marinate the meat for an hour or overnight (while you do other things) in 1 teaspoon sugar, 1 tablespoon cornstarch, 2 tablespoons soy sauce, and 1 cup chicken broth (comes in a can). Stir-fry powdered ginger and garlic (or slices of ginger and minced cloves of garlic) in peanut oil. Stir-fry the meat in this spicy oil until it is brown all over. Add lots of sliced onions, broccoli flowers, fresh green beans snapped in half, and a sprinkle of bran. Add marinade, boil slowly, and stir until thick. Nice with brown rice. Always use common sense. If your family doesn't like ginger, leave it out or substitute a spice or an herb your people do like.

Beef and peas: Soak bite-size pieces of beef in 3 tablespoons soy sauce, 1 tablespoon sesame oil, 1 tablespoon sugar, chopped onion, pepper, garlic and enough cornstarch to thicken. Sauté in vegetable oil. Add twice as many raw peas as you have beef. Smuggle a bit of bran into almost everything you cook. Serve with brown rice, following vegetable h'ors d'oeuvres, and followed by a fruit dessert. Do not make enough of the meat dish for seconds, but serve plenty of everything else.

"Sort of sukiyaki:" Pour 2 tablespoons oil in wok or large frying pan. Add 3 thinly sliced onions, 2 stalks celery sliced diagonally, 3 cups fresh spinach leaves without stems, a bunch of evenly cut scallions, and ½ pound thinly sliced mushrooms. Stir constantly (but only a few minutes) until onions are transparent. Add beef which the butcher has cut into pieces approximately ¼" x 3" and stir quickly for one minute. Add a whole cake of bean curd (buy at Oriental grocery stores listed in the yellow pages and at some supermarkets, or skip it) cut into 1″ cubes. Add ¼ cup soy sauce, ¾ cup bouillon, 1 tablespoon bran and sauté 15 minutes.

Slicing the vegetables is the only slow part of this dinner, but to make this one-dish dinner probably takes no longer than to collect, defrost, unwrap, get water, watch, bake, etc., all the items otherwise necessary to put together a standard family dinner. Each member of the family can, without hardship, slice one vegetable and you almost have an instant dinner. Or invest in a food processor, they're fantastic!

Other Meat-*Less* Dinner and Lunch Ideas

Near eastern lamb: In skillet, slowly sauté 3 pounds cubed (cubed by the butcher) ½″ lamb in corn oil. Transfer lamb to casserole. To skillet, add more oil if necessary, then 3 cups finely chopped onion and 1 cup finely chopped celery. Sauté until vegetables wilt. Add 1 cup bouillon or broth, garlic, thyme, salt, pepper, and bay leaf. Bring to a boil and pour over lamb. Cover casserole and let simmer on stove top 1 hour. Add 1 cup dried lentils, ¼ cup uncooked brown rice, 2 tablespoons bran, and 2 more cups bouillon or broth. Cook one more hour.

There isn't much to *do* about a dish like this, but it does take cooking time. Many dishes of this nature can be made *after* dinner, while parents are home from work and are doing other house chores and child care activities. The *next* evening, they're more instant than any TV frozen dinner—just heat and serve. It takes two minutes to heat a portion of this and put it in a thermos cannister for lunch.

Smorrebrod: If cholesterol isn't a problem, serve any or all of the following at one meal on thickly buttered tiny slices of rye bread. Give each person lots of non-meat open-face sandwiches and only a few with meat.

- Canned or cooked shrimp, lettuce leaf, dab of mayonnaise, topped with lemon slice
- Pickled herring on lettuce with orange-rind trim
- Danish blue cheese (or a cheese the family prefers)
- Caviar with lemon
- Slice of chicken, triangle of pineapple, strawberry or cherry (Don't eat the dyed cherry; it's just for decoration.)
- Smoked salmon, cream cheese
- Blendered chicken liver paté with a cucumber slice
- Danish ham and scrambled egg
- Roast veal with cooked red cabbage and prune
- Sardines, lettuce, lemon
- Raw ground beef with diced onion, horseradish, and mustard all mixed in
- Camembert cheese topped with diced onion and carraway seed

Serve with a special dessert. Bet you guessed—this is a weekend or holiday dinner, not an everyday quickie. But one of the above won't take long and, accompanied by a bag of raw vegetable niblets, makes a fine lunch.

Sesame beef with peanut butter sauce: For two hours, soak beef or veal cubes in ¼ cup soy sauce, garlic, tablespoon chopped onion, ginger. Broil for ½ hour on oiled cookie sheet. Serve with a dip of crunchy peanut butter thinned with peanut oil, soy sauce, lemon juice, and a little skim milk; and with a dish of sesame seeds to roll the sticky cubes in.

Chinese five-spice casserole: Includes meat, but so much less than a "meat, potato and vegetable" standard all-American dinner. Make brown rice according to directions on the package, but add a few bouillon cubes during the last 15 minutes. Sauté lean hamburger or ground veal in corn oil, and add chutney, anise, fennel, cloves and cinnamon. Stir rice and spiced hamburger mix together before serving with a fabulous salad. (This time, you could hide the bran in the salad, like croutons, instead of smuggling it into the casserole.)

Beef relish loaf: Combine 1½ pounds lean beef, ¼ cup wheat germ (or crushed cornflakes or bran) with ¼ cup chopped onion, pepper, and either lots of stuffed green olives or rounds of dill pickle. Serve surrounded with colorful sautéed vegetables. Bake at 350° for 30 or more minutes.

Shishkebob: Marinate cubed lamb in salad dressing. Put on skewers with raw mushrooms, peppers, onions and water chestnuts. (Water chestnuts come in cans and are available at many supermarkets.) On cookie sheet, bake at 350 degrees for an hour. Goes well with brown rice.

Hash: Dice 2 cups any leftover meat and combine with ½ cup diced cooked leftover potatoes, ½ cup diced sautéed onions, and 1 cup canned gravy. Dissolve 2 tablespoons whole-wheat flour in 2 tablespoons 100 percent corn oil margarine. Then add ½ cup tomato pureé, 1 cup water, 1 teaspoon Worchestershire sauce. Pour this mixture into an oiled baking dish, top with wheat germ and cheese, brown at 350 degrees for 15 minutes. An unusual salad will make this a supper or lunch special.

Spoonburgers: Sauté in corn oil 3 cups chopped celery, 3 cups chopped onion, 2 pounds lean ground beef, 2 cans undiluted tomato sauce, and pepper. Serve over wholewheat buns with salad. Any extra can be frozen. A real quickie—fresh or frozen and reheated.

Mixed baked hodge-podge: Put all types of cooked leftovers together in oiled baking dish and mix. These might be spaghetti, rice, potato, meat, vegetables, casseroles—just about anything will work. Stir wheat germ into this and bake till hot and bubbly. Serve with a large, specially good salad.

What do you usually cook for your family? Can some

of your regulars be modified to fit our rules? *Slight changes might make a healthy difference.*

Meal-Big Salads

Chef salad: With soup, special bread, and dessert, this salad: a big bowl of lettuce, romaine, parsley pieces, spinach and any other salad greens liberally covered with slices of cold chicken and mushroom, beef and cheese chunks, tomato quarters, green pepper garnishes, all covered with a favorite dressing (barbecue sauce is delicious) and served with scoop of fresh cottage cheese in the center.

Antipasto: On a platter, arrange a bed of lettuce or other green leaves, then cold boiled potato quarters, black olives, hard boiled egg halves, and highly garlicked chunks of beef (instead of salami). Use a dressing of olive oil, tarragon vinegar, lemon juice, mustard, salt, pepper and garlic. Serve with bread sticks, cheese, fruit and red wine (grape juice for the young).

Aspic: Put 1 envelope plain gelatin into 2 cups of room temperature canned consommé. Let set 5 minutes. Then heat until dissolved and refrigerate until jelled. Serve on salad greens ringed with mounds of miscellany such as hard-boiled egg halves and various chilled canned or cooked vegetables including asparagus tips.

Meat salad: Chop up leftover meat, mix with lots of chopped onion, celery, green pepper, pickle relish, and mayonnaise. Serve on mixed green leaves with a thick soup and interesting bread. Bran bread would be good.

Potato salad: A good place to smuggle in some extra nutrients, and add a little meat for a meat*less* main dish: Dice boiled potatoes, dill pickle, hard boiled egg, leftover meat of any kind, a *lot* of celery, some onion, and a small quantity of raw and green beans, carrot and green pepper (if the family likes it). Throw in a *few raw* green peas. Then hide all in mayonnaise, pickle relish, paprika, pepper, and lemon dressing.

You can also take the fruit ideas from Chapter Nine and make them into tasty salads. See Chapter Thirteen: Fish and Poultry, for tuna and chicken salad recipes.

Make the Month When You Convert to Less Meat More Manageable

Vegetarians and near vegetarians don't have this problem, but many people find that minimizing meat in their diet, especially their *dinner* diet, is one of the most difficult parts of the conversion. May we suggest a method of making the first meatless month easier? Eating less meat will be easier to do with practice.

First Week: Serve pork half as often as you usually do. Substitute veal or chicken in recipes that call for pork, or have something altogether different. Keep this up next week.

Second Week: Serve meat in half as many meals as you usually do. Serve chicken, fish, pasta or bean dishes, soup and salad, or anything other than meat at the other meals. But make them big, tasty, "unprotestable" meals. Continue this.

Third Week: Again cut in half the frequency with which you serve pork. Keep remembering to avoid pork products from now on, or to cut the amounts you're serving every few weeks if it's still too much.

Fourth Week: Cut the number of meat meals in half again, or serve half as much meat at meals: half-size portions of meat with an abundance of everything else. Or, use meat as a mere ingredient in soup, stew, or a casserole. Keep up the good work, and cut a little more each month, if necessary.

Almost All Experts Agree (You'll Never Find 100 Percent on Anything in Life)

Eat less meat. Be good to your cholesterol level. You may not be part of the 50 percent of the population that risks heart disease from high cholesterol levels, but how can you be sure? Besides it seems best to play it safe with your children. You don't know what life holds in store for their hearts. Help them now and in the future through food habits, through the daily diet pattern you are helping them learn. And a fringe benefit for the whole family: eating less meat saves money for far more valuable fruits and vegetables and other fine protein foods. Eat protein, yes, but eat less of it in the form of meat. That's right—eat right, eat less meat. Help the children have happy hearts.

P.S. If you do not like these specific recipes, don't let that fact be a deterrent to trying to implement the general principle: cut meat consumption way, way down.

CHAPTER ELEVEN:

Also Excellent Protein, Eggs and Cheese

When you don't serve meat meals, what *can* you make for dinner?

Eggs

Eggs and cheese contain excellent protein. But eggs are one of the foods that certain nutritionists and many food faddists fight over. No one fights about fruits, and most agree that eating two to four a day—one a citrus fruit—is a good idea. No one fights about vegetables, and most agree it's wise to have some dark green, some deep yellow, and some fibery ones each day. (Those who don't advocate eating these vegetables are usually publicity seekers.) There is some controversy about meat, although it is generally agreed that we eat too much. But, among the experts, eggs cause great controversy.

The majority of authorities strongly favors three or four (but no more) eggs a week *includng those eggs used as invisible ingredients in baked goods, batters, meatloaf, potato salad, sauces, and so on.* Dr. Lawrence Galton, for example, a leading authority on hypertension and heart disease, subscribes to this view. There is excellent protein in eggs, and a lot of lecithin to counteract cholesterol, and fine Vitamin A. That's why experts encourage us to include eggs in our weekly diet.

But eggs are also full of cholesterol—So much so that a minority of nutrition specialists urge us to altogether avoid all eggs in all forms. "Authentic" nutritionists—those with advanced degrees in nutrition and positions of esteem on the nutrition scene—do not suggest that we eat raw or fertile eggs. Though certain self-styled experts make great claims for raw and fertile eggs, including increased valor and virility, the professionals say that raw eggs are less digestable, fertile eggs are more imaginatively priced, and the entire argument is a fetish best left to nonscientific food faddists to cluck over.

Egg Ideas

Few folks want to spend their lives in the kitchen. None of these take long:

Start the children's day with French toast: With a fork, stir up an egg, a teaspoon of sugar, a drop of vanilla, and a sprinkle of nutmeg or cinnamon. Dip a piece of whole-wheat bread in the egg, coating both sides. Then sauté gently in corn oil. Serve with syrup (we can't totally deprive the family of sugar foods).*

Peel whole hard-boiled eggs for breakfast, for the lunch box, or place them prominently in the refrigerator for a snack, with or without salt or a dab of mayonnaise, a favorite with many children.

Deviled eggs—add mayonnaise and mustard to the mashed yolk and stuff the whites (nice on a platter of goodies at a birthday party.)

Make a sliced hard-boiled egg *mini-sandwich,* with or without garnish (mustard butter is a great garnish).

* If children don't eat eggs, eggs can easily be used as an ingredient in something—a blendered milkshake, for example, or hollandaise sauce, crepes, custard, etc. But probably if a parent were to try each of these egg ideas at a rate of one or two a week, he would be surprised to find the children enjoying eggs several ways. It's not necessary to tell egg loathers that the dish features eggs. It also isn't necessary to have children eat eggs. But it doesn't take many above-board and stacked-away egg ideas to get four eggs a week into a child. The probability is that your children already eat too *much* egg, at least as an ingredient.

Try a fried egg on toast sandwich (fry slowly in vegetable oil. What you'll have is really a sautéed egg).

How about an egg-salad sandwich once each week?

Omelettes are easy for breakfast, lunch or dinner. They can be plain, with a slice of cheese melted on top or chopped in. Or include sautéed onion and mushrooms, chervil, chives, tarragon, garlic and so on. The egg mass in an omelette must be very thin, so use a large pan for a little egg liquid and it can spread itself thin. Cook omelettes only for a few seconds. Check cookbooks listed at the end of this book for fabulous omelette recipes.

Put hard-boiled egg halves in cheese cream sauce for a main dish; serve with a home-made bread and a substantial salad.

Eggs flamenco are fancy: Chop potato into a pan with hot olive oil and fry potato briefly. Put potatoes in oiled individual casseroles. Add (in layers) *briefly* cooked peas, pimentos, asparagus (or skip it), and undiluted canned tomato soup. Then, break an egg over the top of each casserole, and bake until the whites have set. Salt and serve.

Spanish omelette: Slowly sauté diced potatoes and onions in olive oil. Beat eggs till foamy and put together with potatoes. Add salt and pepper. Start omelette in olive oil over high heat, then lower heat. Put plate over pan and dump omelette upside down, slide it back into the pan to do the other side. (It sounds time consuming, but takes only 10 minutes.)

Egg foo yong: Put vegetable oil in pan, heat, and add chopped celery (including tops) and chopped scallions. Set aside while blending egg, a touch of honey, and an essence of sweet herbs. Cook covered for a minute. Add some cut-up cooked chicken and the vegetables. Cook only until eggs are firm.

Cheese

Cheese is a dairy product and a protein. Some cheeses contain more fat than others. The less fatty, less caloric cheeses are cottage cheese, hoop cheese, and mozzarella cheese.

The fattiest cheeses are those made from cream or whole milk, such as cheddar and American. The latter are excellent sources of nutrition, if you don't have to guard against calories and cholesterol. Unless they are directed otherwise by a physician, people benefit from eating a few servings of any type of cheese each week.

Processed cheeses contain emulsifiers, stabilizers, and other chemicals which give them their characteristic plastic look and texture. Most nutritionists do not recommend processed cheeses. As with eggs, experts disagree as to whether eating the caloric cheeses every day is a good idea or is excessive. Skim-milk cheese is encouraged as part of the daily diet. Probably it is a good idea for vegetarians to eat cheese higher in animal fats. But nonvegetarians get protein in chicken, fish, and lean meat, so limiting high calorie, high cholesterol cheese to several times a week is very likely wise.

If we're going to stop putting junk foods in children's lunches, yet keep the kids on our side, *we have to put in other goodies:* *

Many teenagers and children like cheese chunks on fancy toothpicks at parties—just plain as a snack or as a while-you-wait-till-I-get-dinner-ready appetizer. A baggie of multi-types of cheese chunks is nice in a lunch bag. So is a cheese, mustard, and black bread sandwich. Swiss cheese, cheddar cheese and American cheese are high in protein, riboflavin, Vitamin A and calcium. A sandwich with one of these cheeses spread with mustard butter or lemon/dill butter is delicious.

* Repeat. We have to replace no-no goodies while we're diminishing and withdrawing good-for-you goodies, or this year-long conversion won't work.

Broiler melted, open-faced cheese sandwiches (skip the frying involved in grilling) with or without tuna, tomatoes, or pickles, are tasty. (One child who loves the book *Heidi* calls these Heidi sandwiches.)

Mix grated cheddar cheese with an equivalent amount of a mixture made of: ¼ cup wheat germ, ⅛ cup ketsup, ⅛ cup mustard, ⅛ cup mayonnaise, and a packet of yeast; spread on toasted whole grain bread and put under broiler until bubbly.

Do things with cottage cheese (also high in protein, riboflavin, vitamin A, and calcium): Serve it plain or with a touch of sugar and milk for dessert. Try an ice-cream scoop of cottage cheese with paprika in it. Put it on lettuce with pear and salad dressing. Stuff it in celery with salt.

To make herbed cottage cheese—add to cottage cheese: dill, thyme, marjoram, parsley, chives, poppy seeds, carraway seeds, sesame seeds, sage, and basil. Use as a cracker spread or celery filler.

Cottage cheese pancakes: For two people, blend together 1 cup cottage cheese, 3 beaten eggs, 1½ tablespoons of vegetable oil, ½ cup whole-wheat flour, salt, ground cumin seeds or other herbs or spices you like. Make wide flat patties and broil in oiled pan. Serve with apricot or raspberry yogurt.

Welsh rarebit, a nice supper dish with salad: In pan, put 100 percent corn oil margarine, yellow cheese, mustard, Worcestershire sauce, a little skim milk, 1 egg yolk. Stir to blend. When hot, thick and blended, serve on whole-wheat toast.

Cream cheese is the least "good" of the cheeses because it's less high than other cheese in valuable nutrients and much higher in fat content. But lots of children love it, and it's a lot better than many foods they eat.*

* In this conversion process, *better* is always preferred to *less* good.

Shredded cheese or a crusty melted cheese topping is tempting and tasty on almost any vegetable.

Lots of children like cheese blintzes: Make a batter of 2 beaten eggs, ¾ cup whole-wheat flour, 1 teaspoon baking powder, ⅔ cup skim milk, ½ cup water, vanilla and 2 tablespoons of honey. Oil a pan, cook a thin "pancake." Make a filling of 2½ cups cottage cheese, 2 beaten egg yolks, 1½ teaspoons 100 percent corn oil margarine, lemon juice, and sugar. Put filling on pancake and roll. Sauté gently on all sides and serve with sour cream and jam.

Cheese can contribute to casseroles, as in cheese potato pie: Peel, quarter, and boil potatoes in the least possible amount of water. Then mash them with milk, margarine, and beaten egg yolks. Whip egg white, add salt, and add to potatoes with seasoning and parsley. Oil a pie plate, sprinkle with wheat germ, put in potato mixture and slices of mozzarella cheese in alternating layers, ending with cheese. Sprinkle with Parmesan cheese and bake for 45 minutes.

Macaroni (whole-wheat) and cheese, or spaghetti (whole-wheat) and cheese in tomato-meat sauce are, of course, long established favorites of children. Extra cheese can be added.

Cheese fondue is made by blending 6 beaten eggs, 3 cups skim milk, 3 cups whole-wheat bread crumbs, 3 cups grated hard yellow cheese, 2 tablespoons vegetable oil, and any herbs you like (marjoram?). Bake at 350 degrees in oiled casserole for half an hour.

For a treat, try cheese surprise loaf (children like surprises): In a bread pan, make a vegetable loaf. When it's nearly baked, remove the loaf to a cookie tin. Cover it with sheets of cheese, and melt in oven. To make the loaf: combine mashed potatoes blended with wheat germ and blendered cooked carrots and spinach, blendered raw onion, plus chopped celery and parsley. In the middle, hide several whole, shelled, hard-boiled eggs.

For a cheesy party casserole, to be served with a spectacular salad and fancy fruit dessert, make Cheese and Mushroom cap casserole: Remove stems (discard or use for something else) and sauté in corn oil only the caps of 1 pound of mushrooms. Add Worcestershire sauce, pepper and garlic. Separately, make a cheese sauce: Melt 4 tablespoons corn oil margarine, add 2 tablespoons whole-wheat flour and stir till blended. Slowly pour in skim milk, stirring and thickening until sauce reaches consistency you like. Add as much chopped cheddar cheese as desired. When it has been stirred and blended till smooth, pour the sauce over the mushrooms, which have been attractively arranged in a pie tin or shallow casserole, and bake at 350 degrees for 25 minutes.

A good way to get cheese and eggs into the family's weekly diet without feeding folks excessive doses of cholesterol is to prepare pre-dinner cheese or egg h'ors d'oeuvres, and then feature poultry or bean meals, which are highly recommended for high protein, low cholesterol foods. Everybody loves h'ors d'oeuvres; they lend a festive note to family suppers.

CHAPTER TWELVE:

Highly Recommended Protein Foods: Poultry and Fish

Eat Unlimited Amounts of Poultry

The light meat of chicken and turkey without the skin is very low in fats (calories, cholesterol) and high in protein. Many tasty dishes can be made of chicken and turkey. Eating the skin is not a sin, but the skin does contain fat. Eating the dark meat is roughly equivalent to eating beef. Except for proponents of vegetarianism, no diet specialists oppose the consumption of large amounts of chicken and turkey. Chicken and turkey are considered excellent foods by nutritionists.

Cookbooks are full of recipes for broiled, roasted, baked, and fried chicken, chicken salad, chicken soup, etc. Sliced chicken sandwiches with mayonnaise or mustard on dark bread, or a thermos of chicken soup are nice lunches.

Some favorite recipes follow. All can be used as lunch food (leftover from a dinner earlier in the week):

Chicken mozzarella: Dredge chicken in whole-wheat flour, salt, and pepper. Sauté in vegetable or olive oil with garlic and chopped onion; pour into baking pan on top of canned tomatoes and put more tomatoes on top of chicken. Also add tomato paste, oregano, garlic, pepper, and sliced olives. Cover with a mozzarella cheese slice, bake at 350 degrees for an hour. Serve with a simple salad.

Chicken vegarella: Using low heat, sauté chicken rolled in whole-wheat flour in vegetable oil. Then add chopped raw parsley, carrot, onion, mushrooms, celery, tomato and eggplant, garlic, salt, and pepper. Cover and simmer until chicken is tender. Serve with brown rice or brown noodles.

Cheddar chicken: Sauté boned or regular chicken in vegetable oil. Cook two packages of French green beans or broccoli as usual (*briefly!*). Put vegetable on bottom of oiled baking dish and chicken on top of it. To a can of condensed cheddar cheese soup, add cayenne, and pour over chicken. Sprinkle with whole-wheat bread crumbs, bacon bits, and ½ cup of shredded cheddar cheese. Broil until brown and bubbly. Because it's rich, it's well-followed by fresh fruit.

Puerto Rican pollo: Brown chicken in vegetable oil. Put in deep pot. Brown chunks of fresh tomatoes, onion, carrot, potato and celery in the same oil. Add salt, pepper, garlic, oregano, bay leaf and tomato paste. Combine all in pot and bake until soft. Serve with brown rice or brown noodles.

Dunked drumsticks: Blend 1 tablespoon mustard, 1 teaspoon Worchestershire sauce and ½ cup skim milk. Dunk 16 skinned drumsticks in it. Roll them in ½ cup wheat germ with pepper. Place in shallow, foil-lined pan. Bake at 350 degrees for 1½ hours. Before serving, wrap ends in fringed 3″ strips of foil or cellophane so people can conveniently hold their drumsticks while dunking them in a sauce of mustard, ketsup, and relish.* A fine event for somebody's birthday.

Club sandwich: Combine mayonnaise and mustard, and spread on whole-wheat toast. Add slowly fried bacon, tomato, lettuce, and toast with more mayonnaise on top. Add slices of cooked chicken and cucumber. Top

---

* Ketsup relish contains sugar. But we are not perfectionists. If children gradually stop drinking soft drinks and artificial fruit "drinks," and stop eating candy bars, store cookies, cakes, cupcakes, pies, syrups, so much jam and jelly, so much ice cream, and so on, we won't have to worry about a little sugar in the ketsup.

with a third piece of toast. (Yes, bacon, but if you eat only the amount of bacon included in recipes in this book, you'll only be eating 5 or 6 slices a season.) How about a homemade soup to complete this supper?

Creamed chicken: Melt 100 percent corn oil margarine, thicken with whole-wheat flour, and add skim milk and non-instant milk powder.* Simmer until you have cream sauce. Add lots of pieces of leftover cooked chicken and mushroom slices sautéed in velegtable oil. Season to taste with herbs. Serve with brown rice, salad, and fruit.

Poulet: Roast a chicken or chicken parts. Meanwhile, put into pan ¼ cup water, ½ teaspoon butter or corn oil, ½ teaspoon lemon juice, salt, and one pound sliced mushrooms. Cover and boil slowly for 8 minutes. Pour out liquid and save. Mix 1 cup skim milk, salt, pepper, and enough cornstarch or whole-wheat to thicken into 2 tablespoons butter and pour over mushrooms. Simmer 2 minutes. Remove chicken from its pan, put onion or shallot into the drippings, add the mushroom juice, add mushrooms and sauce. Simmer, add lemon, stir. Try with a non-rich vegetable casserole on the side.

Roast chicken: Rub chicken with 100 percent corn oil margarine and salt. Roast for 30 minutes, add chicken broth, raw onion or shallot, and carrot. Add tarragon and lemon to the juices and baste.

Chicken a la almond: Bake pieces of chicken or a whole chicken and serve with cream sauce. To make the cream sauce, melt 100 percent corn oil margarine, add whole-wheat flour, and stir till blended. Add skim milk and stir. Then add slivered almonds, almond extract, and nutmeg. An exotic salad will round out the meal.

---

* There are two kinds of milk powder. One says instant on the box. Many brands don't mix well when heated. The other kind *doesn't* say instant. It mixes well under a wider variety of circumstances.

Chicken a la king for 8: Dice 2 cups cooked chicken and set aside. Sauté 1 cup sliced mushrooms and ½ cup canned pimento in vegetable oil. Thicken oil with whole-wheat flour after scooping out solids. Add 3 cups clear chicken soup or bouillon (buy it canned or make it), add everything; serve on whole-wheat toast, toasted whole-wheat hamburger buns, or brown rice. An interesting raw vegetable platter would go well with this.

Sweet and sour roast chicken: Sauté mushrooms in vegetable oil. Make a sauce by adding sauerkraut, canned pineapple chunks, and water chestnuts to mushrooms. Then pour this sauce over a chicken for last 15 minutes of its roasting. There are very few calories in this trimly delicious little number. (Another way to make this a weightwatcher dish is to substitute bean sprouts for sauerkraut, and mustard for mushrooms.)

Yogurt chicken: Brush pieces of chicken with vegetable oil and put in casserole; surround with sliced onions. Pour on a sauce of melted margarine, thickened with whole-wheat flour, to which tarragon, parsley, and chicken broth have been added. Cover and bake at 350° for 1 hour. Blend yogurt into the sauce and serve with two "straight up" vegetable favorites.

You name it chicken: Spread chicken pieces in bottom of well oiled deep casserole. Cover with raw bacon bits. Mix 1 box frozen peas, 1 box frozen French green beans, sliced green pepper, onion, lots of sliced mushrooms, and spread on top. Bake at 350° for 1½ hours. The juices make a tasty sauce. Serve with homemade biscuits.

California chicken salad: Cube cold baked chicken and put it in a bowl with avocado chunks, tomato, cucumber, lettuce and walnuts. Stir in lime dressing (lime juice, olive oil, garlic, salt, pepper) and serve on bed of various fresh, crisp greens. Marvelous with tasty, newly baked bread and fruit spread.

Easy Does It

Far from being inordinately time consuming, any of the recipes above, and any of the meals described in the meat*less* chapter, can be SOS meals—the type you freeze ahead to serve when a hungry family wants food *now* and parents got home late from work. Or when guests drop in unexpectedly. It takes no longer to shove one of these casserole dishes in the oven and thaw it to succulence, than it does to thaw and heat tacky TV dinners. Not one of the chicken dinners discussed here takes more than 25 minutes actual preparation time, though all take more time to cook. Most parents are in the house that long each day, at least on weekends, and can tuck the making and freezing of these family-pleasing delectables in around other chores and joys.

If you have a meat meal once a week, a meat*less* meal once a week, a cheese or egg meal once a week, and poultry twice a week, you only have two dinner menues left to plan. Perhaps fish for one and a legume, nut or seed main dish for the other?

Children Raised on Fish Eat Fish

Babies, toddlers, and little children who are served fish in many forms usually grow into children and adults who will eat or really enjoy fish. Fish has as much protein as meat has, but much less fat.* The trouble with serving fish is that unless there are good fishermen in the family or a fresh fish store nearby, people must eat the narrow selection of (usually frozen) fish available at the supermarket or go to a great deal of trouble to get fresh fish. Any food project that makes boring eating or requires lots of trouble is going to rank low on many people's lists of how they want to treat their families or invest their time.

* Some of the fatter fish are salmon, trout, shad, herring, and mackerel, but even they don't have half the fat contained in the same amount of beef.

However, for those people who can get fish without too much hassle (some fresh fish stores deliver) and for people who can get some kinds of fresh or frozen fish at the supermarket, here are some varieties of fish foods that take the dull out of a fish dinner. Children who have not grown up on fish can get used to these dishes and may (surprise, surprise) love them. For a beginning, we can aim at serving fish for one meal every other week. Then, fish can be served more frequently after the family becomes fond of it.

Fishy Suggestions

Bake fish (till a meat thermometer, inserted in the thickest part of the fish, reaches 150 degrees, or until it flakes). If it's cooked more, fish gets dry and also makes the house smell fishy. Before or after baking:

- Brush with vegetable oil, and add butter, lemon, salt, and pepper.
- Stuff with rice, mushrooms, celery, onion, and the like, that have first been sautéed in vegetable oil.
- Put paprika all over the fish before baking so it will turn brown.
- Before baking, dip it in milk (which kills all odor) and wheat germ * (found in the store with cereals).

* Wheat germ looks like grapenuts or bread crumbs. It's an excellent source of the B vitamins, protein, and vitamin E, and can easily be added to foods as a filler (in meat loaf, stews, casseroles, vegetable dishes, baked goods, etc.) or to give crunch (roll meat, fish, or vegetables in it before sautéing, and soon). But it's no more essential to eat wheat germ, as food fadists would have us believe, than to eat any other food. For example, the same B vitamins abound in liver, and lots of foods have more protein than wheat germ does: lentils, legumes, some seeds, dry peas, soy beans, ground nuts, and nonfat milk powder (another excellent filler—no one will notice if we sneak it into foods and milk drinks to fortify them). Even those old-fashioned foods like cheese, meat, and fish have fine protein. Nonetheless, wheat germ is a wonderfully healthy and convenient food and nutrient extender to have in the house as a staple.

- Dip it in barbecue sauce before baking.
- Over the fish, put cream sauce made of 100 percent corn oil margarine, milk, whole-wheat flour—plain, or with dill, or with cheese, oregano and garlic.
- Bake in layers with alternate layers of onion and pickle.
- Bake in sweet-and-sour sauce made of stock (bouillon will do) containing soy sauce, ginger, mace, cinnamon, nutmeg, allspice, bay leaf, ¼ cup vinegar (sour), ¼ cup molasses (sweet), grated onion, raisins, almonds, wheat flour to thicken. Heat the sauce slowly and boil briefly to thicken before adding to fish.
- Serve fish hot with a sauce of heated ketsup, lemon juice, Worcestershire sauce, horseradish, and vinegar to taste.
- Bake salmon (bright pink and very pretty). Then marinate it (soak it) overnight and serve it cold.

To make the marinade, mix 3 sliced onions, 3 cups water, ½ cup vinegar, lots of lemon juice, 1 teaspoon pickling spice, bay leaf, lots of black pepper, and boil 2 minutes.

The best way to bake fish is on a lightly oiled rack above something to catch the drip, with nothing touching the underside but the rack. The fishy smell can be kept off hands with rubber gloves, or can be removed by washing hands in soda.

Fish can be broiled. Here are a few things to do with broiled fish.

- Ahead of time, brush fish with oil, either well-rolled in dill or tarragon or plain. Serve with butter, salt, and lemon added at end.
- Cut into sticks first, then roll in cornmeal and sauté in vegetable oil for a minute before broiling. Fish sticks are a favorite with many children. Some like them dunked in ketsup.
- For fish kebabs, marinate chunks of fish in lemon

and oil salad dressing, spiked with chervil, bacon,* mushrooms, onions, and green pepper. Put on skewer. Broil until fish is done.

- Pour a mixture of dill, Dijon mustard and olive oil over broiled fish.
- Serve broiled fish with this parsley butter sauce: 3 parts real butter melted, 1 part finely chopped parsley, juice of 3 lemons, salt, cayenne pepper. (Sardines are fish: make a sardine sandwich with parsley butter spread; make it as just described, but don't melt the butter.)

Frying or deep frying fish adds a great many calories and a lot of fat. Excess fat is undersirable for many people because of its cholesterol, and most people can do without excess calories. However, since lightly, quickly pan fried fresh fish are so delicious, we may decide that this is one of the treats, or exceptions, we want from time to time. In a pan, put enough butter (this is an exception too) or margarine to equal half the thickness of the fish. When the butter is hot, put in the fish that has been rolled in wheat germ. The fish should be taken out as soon as it's golden, and is done in the middle—test with a fork for whiteness or flakiness. Fish also tastes good and is nourishing when it has been rolled in cornmeal or whole-wheat flour, herbed or plain.

After baking or broiling, fish can be added to an otherwise finished casserole for a delicious dinner. For example:

Fish delish: Slightly sauté diced carrots, pepper, onion, and tomato (all can be rolled in herbs or wheat germ first). Add fish when ready to serve—just toss the mixture a little bit.

Saucy fish: Cover fish with cream sauce containing briefly cooked peas, diced green beans, potatoes, leeks,

---

* Getting away from regularly eating bacon for breakfast, BLTs for lunch, and bacon-laden dinner dishes doesn't mean one will never use a bit of bacon as an ingredient.

and whatever (preferably colorful) vegetables your family likes.

Pot pies: Take either one of the two combinations just listed; put into individual foil tart tins. Cover with pie crust and bake.

Make fish patties with previously cooked and mashed fish, mixed with wheat germ, dill, and raw egg. Sauté the patties slowly and serve with lemon and tartar sauce.

Make fish loaf of cooked fish, any chopped vegetables (fresh or leftover) including parsley and onion. Add eggs and skim milk until the loaf sticks together. Bake for 45 minutes in a loaf pan oiled and sprinkled with wheat germ (hide the loaf under melted cheese if children "don't eat" fish).

Lots of children like chilled fish cocktails—it's the cocktail glasses and red sauce they find appealing: Flake cooked fish, put in cocktail glasses with a sauce made of lemon juice, salt, pepper, and ketsup. Or use chili sauce or barbecue sauce and horseradish.

Marinated herring is fish; try it as an h'ors d'oeuvre.

Curried fish: Sauté fish in vegetable oil with tumeric; add ginger, curry, paprika, parsley, oregano, fresh tomato, fresh green pepper, slivered almonds and water and cook until the mixture has a good texture.

Seafood salad: Mix one cup chopped green pepper, half cup chopped onion, 2 cups chopped celery, 2 cups mayonnaise, 2 cans crabmeat, 2 cans shrimp, and 2 cans white tuna fish. Mix in a little mayonnaise, Worcestershire sauce, and a dash of tabasco. If you're following a low cholesterol regimen, leftover fish is fine for salads. Serve with homemade rolls and a rich dessert.

Three favorites with nonfish eaters are:

Jambalaya (children have been known to eat it because they like the name). In a pan, put these ingredients and simmer covered until lightly cooked: cooked brown rice, flaked fish, bacon bits, grated onion, chopped pepper, canned or fresh tomatoes, onion, herbs such as basil or oregano, celery seed, garlic, and stock.

Tuna is an excellent source of protein, and many children will happily eat a tuna sandwich or salad a number of times a week (sneak vegetables into it—chopped green pepper, celery, or onion).

Tuna and noodles: Boil noodles or macaroni; put in oiled baking dish. Cover with sauce made by melting 100 percent corn oil margarine and blending in wholewheat flour, skim milk, chopped cheese, and plenty of tuna fish. Sprinkle with wheat germ and grated cheese. Bake at 350 for 15 minutes.

Cookbooks are full of fish soups, bisques and chowders, but here are several to start off with. If yours is not already a fish-eating family, you may want to serve these soups as openers to meals your family is accustomed to. After people get used to them, serve this type of fish dish as the supper's centerpiece, with salad, special bread, and dessert.

Fish bisque: Make this thick milk soup by boiling fish of any kind in water with onion and nutmeg. Pour an equal amount of milk into the liquid. Thicken the bisque with a paste of heated margarine, whole-wheat flour, pepper and herbs. Put through blender.

Fish chowder: Combine these ingredients in pot: corn oil, chopped onion, sage, marjoram, parsley, garlic, water and canned tomatoes. Simmer until onion is transparent and celery is tender. Then add *cooked* fish of one or many kinds, stir together, and serve hot.

Besides serving fish dishes on the side for awhile, another technique found by many to be effective in helping the family switch to fish is to make only enough for the family members who *like* fish, making it far-

and-away the most attractive dish on the table. Serve a dull but familiar supper to the rest of the family, and apologize that there isn't enough of the main event for everyone. Scarcity creates demand (sometimes).

Shellfish

It has been thought by scientists specializing in food that shellfish—oysters, clams, crabs, lobsters, shrimp and scallops—are low in calories (fat) but are high in cholesterol. Physicians have usually recommended that people on low-fat, low-cholesterol meal plans eat shellfish no more than twice a month. New findings suggest that some shell fish may *not* be high in cholesterol. If interested, write to the National Institutes of Health, Cholesterol Research, Bethesda, Maryland and find out.

CHAPTER THIRTEEN:

Highly Recommended Protein, Legumes, Nuts and Seeds

Why Eat Legumes, Nuts and Seeds?

Some people don't believe in killing animals and eating meat. Others don't want to consume gobs of cholesterol in meat. Still others want to spend less money on groceries, either because they don't have the money, because they want to spend it for things other than eating, or because they're trying to de-escalate their cost of living so they can earn less, work less, and become more involved in childraising, work, or special interests.

Some are concerned about the fact that our small, overpopulated planet may run out of food for its people; they believe we need to use what nature produces more economically. It *is* possible to forget meat altogether and still eat in a healthy, high protein way. But even among the many people who fully intend to continue consuming and relishing meat, there are those who are trying to *limit* their intake for one or another of the above reasons.

Protein Is Protein

Part of each human body is made of protein. The body cannot make some of the kinds of amino acids that are in protein. In order to support all of our vital processes, we must feed protein to our cells every day. In other words, we have to eat protein daily for maximal functioning. Because no protein food contains all the amino acids we need, it's important to eat a variety of protein foods.

However, whether the protein and amino acids come from meat or from protein-rich legumes, nuts, seeds, or dairy products doesn't matter. Protein is protein, and amino acids are amino acids, whether they occur in meat or elsewhere. Moreover, adding brewer's yeast (different from regular yeast) or wheat germ as an "additive" to regular recipes fortifies them with further protein.

Some protein-high foods have more calories than others, but the importance of eating protein outweighs the importance of keeping down calories, and besides, *it isn't possible to gain weight on protein foods if only reasonable amounts are eaten.* Fish and dairy products (cottage cheese, yogurt, milk, cheese), meat, and poultry have lots of protein per calorie, but so do legumes (lentils, soybeans, lima beans, kidney beans, split peas, chick peas, black-eye peas, and other such beans and peas). Whole-grain foods and certain vegetables, including broccoli, spinach, asparagus, cauliflower, mushrooms, and others contain some protein, too. Nuts and seeds are high in protein, but many are also high in cholesterol and calories (cashews and walnuts, for example). Nuts and seeds high in protein but *not* high in cholesterol and not too high in calories for the benefit a big handful provides are pumpkin, sunflower, and squash seeds, peanuts and peanut butter.

Protein Complementarity

Diet for a Small Planet and *Recipes for a Small Planet* are two go-together books by two women which show how certain protein foods, when served at the same meal, complement each other so as to provide a good balance of amino acids. The authors offer a rough formula the cook can keep in mind:

• Whole grains and legumes = balance
• Whole grains and milk products = balance
• Legumes and seeds = balance

In other words, for balanced protein, if you serve a whole-grain dish, serve legumes or milk foods as well; if you serve legumes, serve whole grain or seed foods with them. Protein complementarity is the concept of combining the proper preparations of grains, legumes, seeds, and dairy foods to produce a high quality of complete protein.

Liberation From Food "Product Manufacturers"

These days, many people feel liberated from expensive, unhealthy, automated, and fattening family feeding patterns, when they reject most of the plastic or nonfoods and food "products" (??) that slippery TV, slick magazines, and smoothly bright supermarkets display and labels urge us all to eat. It's back to foods produced by earth, sun, and rain, and away from many of those produced by food manufacturers. A sense of freedom and peace fill the mind as more nearly natural foods fill the belly. Fanaticism is not a necessary ingredient of better eating. Freedom means choosing, not just being programmed to eat what the food industry gloatingly finds it profitable to stuff into us (or what the health-food faddists firmly insist we eat either).

As Ellen Buchman Ewald says in *Recipes for a Small Planet,* we still have some choice about what we eat. Each of us has only one body, and we may choose to nourish our body with the foods that grow in the earth, or we may choose to have someone else process our food, add chemicals to it, color it, flavor it, mold it, shape it, preserve it, put it into a plastic bag, put that plastic bag into a box, cover the box with more plastic, put a pretty price on it, tell us that it will taste good, "and most incredibly tell us that it is good food that will sustain our bodies when we eat it!"

Many of us have selected and like lifestyles which do not permit time or provide space to grow our own food, or time to go to great lengths preparing each meal. Yet we can avoid most processed, ridiculously packaged, phony foods, and can buy more old-fashioned, nonwrapped, nature-wrapped, or briefly wrapped items. Simple, beautiful, wholesome meals on attractively set tables can make us feel elegant. And, of course, they're delicious.

In addition to other reasons, we will be contributing to solving the solid-waste problem instead of to the problem itself, when we stop buying so much packaging materials which we rip off, throw into the trash, and worry (or let someone else worry) about recycling.

How to Find Protein Alternatives to Meat

First, go through your recipe collection to find legume dishes that are already familiar favorites. Or, look for dishes that you can modify, by subtracting and adding appropriately, so that they become legume dishes.

Generally, dried beans of any kind need to soak 6 hours or overnight in water before they're cooked. Extra soaked beans can be kept in the refrigerator for a week or so. For shoppers, cooks, and eaters not used to some of the following legume, nut, and seed dishes, *one a week, served as a main or side dish,* is the best beginning. *Alter all recipes to suit the taste of the eaters.*

Secondly, decide whether you want to get used to the trouble of using dried beans and peas, or if you want to compromise—more legumes, less meat, but you'll use "already ready" canned beans and peas.

This book is assuming the latter, but listed cookbooks show how to do it the longer way. This book is for people who aren't passionately interested in cooking, but like good, real food.

Soybean casserole: Place in an oiled baking dish 1 cup corn, 1 cup cooked soybeans,* 1 cup drained tomatoes, salt, paprika, grated onion, a little brown sugar, a lot of bran, 3 tablespoons corn oil, bay leaf, chopped parsley, and thyme. Sprinkle top with wheat germ,

---

* To cook soybeans, plunge in boiling water, cook 2 minutes, let stand one hour, proceed with recipe.

chopped peanuts, cheese. Bake 45 minutes at 350. Serve with leafy, light salad.

Soybean stew: Combine 1 cup dry cooked soybeans, handful bran, one 8-ounce can tomato sauce, 1 stalk chopped celery, ⅓ cup chopped onions, 1 clove crushed garlic or garlic powder, spices to taste (cinnamon, cloves, nutmeg, cumin). Stew ½ hour in heavy, lidded pot. Add chicken bouillon as needed if stew becomes dry. Cover with slices of cheese; put lid on, and leave covered and steaming until cheese melts. Good with salad and a light fruit dessert. This stew is heavy.

Kidney bean stew: Sauté onions in oil. Pour into casserole with partially drained canned kidney beans and an equal amount of canned tomatoes. Add garlic, bran, salt, pepper. If you don't object to bacon as an occasional ingredient, some crisp bacon bits add interest to this dish.

Summer bean salad (the main dish of a summer supper): Put canned, drained red kidney beans, black beans, and chick peas or French green beans in a bowl. make dressing separately by stirring together lemon juice, yogurt, milk powder, curry (optional), chives, bran, parsley, and peppers. Pour dressing over beans and chill. Nice with homemade biscuits.

Baked bean salad: Combine a can of pork and beans, ¼ cup cheddar-cheese chunks, ½ cup chopped sweet pickles, ½ cup chopped celery, chopped onion to taste, bran, salt, and chili powder. Serve chilled on lettuce.

Bean loaf (serve when you're in the mood for meat loaf): Cook 1½ cups any kind of beans (pinto, lima, chick peas, black beans, etc.). Sauté chopped onion in oil, mix together, and add 2 grated carrots, sesame seeds, bran, herbs to taste, salt, pepper, and two beaten eggs. Then bake in oiled casserole or meat loaf pan at 350 degrees for an hour. Pour on a favorite meat loaf sauce. Quite likely, no one will even notice that you're converting to legumes.

Bean stroganoff: Heat 4 tablespoons oil, sauté 1½ cups chopped onion, 3 cups chopped mushrooms. Stir in ¼ cup whole-wheat flour. Then stir in 1 cup water or the vitamin-filled water in which you cooked any vegetables previously or beef bouillon. Add 2 teaspoons Worcestershire sauce, 2 teaspoons mustard, and nutmeg. Just before serving, stir in 1½ cups yogurt and pour over cooked lima beans.

Nut patties: Grind peanuts (1½ cups) in blender; mix with ½ cup sunflower seeds. Then blenderize 2 eggs plus 2 onions and add this liquid to nut-and-seed mixture. Add ¾ cup wheat germ the usual smidgeon of bran, and herbs to taste (sage, thyme, parsley, etc.). Make patties. Sauté in oil. Serve with a homemade fruit pie, or something so special that people are distracted from these new nut patties enough to eat and fall in love with them.

Nut and seed salad: Add chopped peanuts and sunflower seeds, plus raisins, grated cheese, pineapple chunks, a little bran, salt and pepper, to cottage cheese. Put in center of lettuce and raw spinach bed. Surround with colorful cold leftover vegetables, and pour favorite dressing over all. Needs hot bread with a good spread.

Sesame beans: Drop contents of 2 boxes frozen French green beans or the equivalent into a *small* amount of rapidly boiling water and lid. After beans have thawed, drain and combine them with chopped onion, 2 tablespoons bran and 2 tablespoons whole-wheat flour. Stir in 1 cup yogurt and 1 teaspoon honey. Put into oiled deep casserole. Cover with 2 cups grated cheese (any kind you like) and sprinkle thickly with toasted sesame seeds which have first been rolled in oil. Bake at 325 for 30 minutes.

Chile con carne: Heat 4 tablespoons corn oil, sauté 1 cup thinly sliced onions in it. Add 1 pound hamburger and stir over medium heat till brown. Add 1½ cups water, 2 cups canned tomatoes, 3 tablespoons chili powder, 2 teaspoons bran, 2 teaspoons sugar, dash of salt, and garlic. Cover and cook over low heat for 1 hour. Add 4 cups canned kidney beans and cook 30 minutes. Serves 8

Boston baked beans: Boil 2 cups previously soaked dry navy beans for 2 minutes. Remove from heat and let stand for an hour. Add salt and cook slowly for an hour. Then chop ½ small onion and mix with ¼ cup brown sugar, ½ cup molasses, handful bran, and 2 teaspoons mustard; stir mixture into beans. Put in baking pan, cover pan, and bake at 350 for 2 hours, first adding enough water to cover beans if not already wet enough. (You can use baked canned beans instead of dry navy beans.) Either way, beans go well with canned Boston brown bread.

Broiled soyburgers: Blend and make into burgers 2 cups cooked and puréed soybeans, ¼ cup cooked brown rice, garlic, 1 grated carrot, 1 stalk celery and tops, ¼ cup chopped wheat germ, 2 beaten eggs, ½ cup chicken broth, 3 tablespoons oil, dill seeds. Broil until brown.

Serve these soups with salad and whole grain bread or dessert, and you have a nutritious, delicious supper.

Peanut soup: Put 3 tablespoons oil in pan, and, over a low flame, stir in bran, ½ cup chopped onions, ½ cup chopped celery, 2 tablespoons whole wheat flour, one quart clear chicken broth, and celery seed. Simmer 25 minutes, covered, over low flame. Add 1 cup smooth peanut butter, a little at a time, while stirring. Then add 2 teaspoons of lemon juice and 1 cup milk.

Black bean soup: Buy it and serve it as is, or zing it up with chopped onion sautéed in oil, garlic, and dry mustard. Garnish each bowl of soup with half a hard-boiled egg floating in it and put a lemon wedge on the edge of the bowl.

Barley soup (with curry if desired): Cook 1½ cups raw barley according to directions on package. Sauté onion in oil and add barley. Stir 2 cups yogurt into ¼ cup water. Beat 4 eggs, slowly thicken with 2 tablespoons wholewheat flour, and add to yogurt water. Cook on hot flame, stirring till thick but not boiling. Stir in barley and onions. Add chopped parsley and herbs to taste.

Spiced pea soup: Boil 1 cup dried split peas and 4 medium-sized potatoes with peel on (cut in eighths) in 2 quarts water. Meanwhile, over a low flame, in a small pan with oil to cover bottom, mix 1 teaspoon mustard, ½ teaspoon cumin, teaspoon bran, ¾ teaspoon salt. Pour spice mixture into soup. Strain mixture or put through blender. Or, eat as is.

Some more good foods:

Sunflower beans: Drop 1 pound cut green beans into enough rapidly boiling water to cover, boil 2 to 4 minutes. Put corn oil, ½ cup sunflower seeds, a touch of bran, salt, and pepper in frying pan, and heat and stir. Add drained beans while stirring, and serve immediately as a side dish.

Pignoli nut beans (also a side dish): Cook 1 package frozen French green beans as usual. Blenderize ¾ cup olive oil, 3 tablespoons wine vinegar, pepper, basil, oregano, bay leaf, garlic, and ¼ cup grated Parmesan cheese. Put this mixture in skillet with beans and sauté. Sprinkle liberally with pignoli nuts (pine nuts) and serve hot or cold.

Lentil paté: Boil 1½ cups dried lentils 40 minutes or until soft. Put lentils through blender with lemon juice and soy sauce to taste. Meanwhile, sauté 2 small diced onions, garlic and ½ cup chopped parsley in oil. Dampen 3 slices whole-wheat toast in water until soggy and stir into onion mixture. Add pinch of thyme, coriander, celery seed, chili powder, 2 tablespoons dill, salt, pepper, and a beaten egg. Mix the mixture. Bake in an oiled pan for ½ hour at 300 degress. Serve on whole-grain crackers as an h'ors d'oeuvres with a soup, salad, and dessert.

What's So Good About Beans and Nuts?

Beans and nuts contain a lot of magnesium which evidently helps reduce the likelihood of arterial diseases. Whole grains and beans such as soy beans, lima beans, etc., and molasses, are good sources of iron. Beans and nuts contain trace minerals which our bodies must have.

Beans and nuts are a good source of vitamin B_1 (thiamin) and protein. (Rye bread, brewer's yeast and wheat germ—good nutrients to add unobtrusively to many foods—are also good sources of this B vitamin. People who didn't used to get enough B_1 got beriberi disease). Peanuts, as well as fish and meat, contain vitamin B_3 (niacin). Deficiency of niacin results in pellagra.

Brown rice, while not capable of furnishing the body with all needed nutrients as some "dieteers" would have us believe, is a delicious and nutritious staple, from which many a fine meal can be made. A few nice rice ideas:

Slightly Chinese fried (brown) rice: In a large frying pan or wok, heat 3 tablespoons corn oil. Sauté 2 diced scallions, 1 stalk chopped celery till golden. Add 2 cups cooked rice, stirring constantly for about 5 minutes. Beat 2 eggs, add ¼ cup skim milk, soy sauce and nutmeg to taste, and chopped parsley. Pour the mixture into the rice. Stir and serve.

Somewhat Cuban (brown) rice: Cook 2 cups rice. Meanwhile, sauté 4 chopped onions in olive oil till golden. Add 4 cloves of garlic. Add 3 sliced green peppers, 5 cut-up tomatoes, ½ pound sliced mushrooms, oregano, pepper, and hot red pepper if you like it. When all vegetables are tender, mix and serve.

Iranian-Style (brown) rice: Cook 4 cups rice, and preheat oven to 350 degrees. Oil bottom of casserole; cover with thin slices of 3 raw potatoes with peel, and pour oil over them. Spread rice on top. Sprinkle with 1 cup raisins or currants or some of each. Pour more oil over this, cover, bake for 15 minutes; pour into another dish so the bottom becomes the top. Then take off potatoes and save for some other purpose. Serve.

Sort-of-Indian (brown) rice: Prepare rice as directed on package and sauté in curried vegetable oil, with powdered cloves, cinnamon, and nutmeg. Serve each of the following in a separate small bowl: cucumbers in heavy yogurt, shredded coconut, chutney, chopped tomatoes, chopped nuts (peanuts, almonds, or cashews), raisins and any other fruit (fresh, preferably), raw onion or scallion.

Chilled sweet-and-sour herb (brown) rice: Cook and cool 1 cup raw brown rice. Put in serving bowl with 1 large cucumber, sliced, and 1 sliced banana. Stir in some raisins and chopped peanuts. Add a dressing of olive oil, lemon juice, honey, coriander, cumin, and cayenne pepper.

Notes on Nuts and Seeds

Nuts and seeds provide nourishing protein, B vitamins, and necessary roughage. Certain nuts also provide polyunsaturated fats, which bodies badly need. These *good* fats are found in fish, corn oil, and most nuts. Nuts are high in calories, but eating a modest handful or the equivalent each day is a healthy practice. (A handful of nuts is much less bad and much more nourishing than a handful of many other snack foods.) *Some* nuts also provide *too much cholesterol* and *too many calories to make it wise to eat them often.* Cashew and Macedonian nuts are less desirable than other nuts.

If You Aren't a Squirrel, What Can You Do
With Nuts and Seeds?

Well, first off, there's peanut butter. Since almost every child in the U.S.A. knows full well what to do with peanut butter, we won't mention it except in certain novel capacities. For instance, you could put out peanut butter dip and raw vegetables to dunk in it. Begin leaving small bowls of pecans, peanuts, almonds, sesame and sunflower seeds, or popcorn popped in corn oil without much salt, around where and when family snackers usually snack. These foods can be placed on the table where a child arriving home from school will make his landing. While he gears up to get into all the goodies in the refrigerator, he'll very likely start filling up on peanuts, sesame and sunflower seeds, popcorn, peanut butter dip (and fantastic protein!).

Reducing junk food in the diet and eventually nearly dropping it altogether, will be much easier if *other* snacks are attractively available.

Another thing to do with nuts and seeds is to buy or make them into *meal,* and let them "hitchhike" along with the other foods people are eating.

• Secretly sprinkle the meal into loaf and pattie mixtures, into or on top of casseroles, soups, stews, vegetable side dishes, and so on.
• Nuts and seeds, whole, chopped or ground into meal, are delicious in many salads.
• Add nut and seed meal to any bread or baked dessert you're making.
• Put ground peanuts or pecans in pancake batter made with whole-wheat flour.

Nuts and seeds can be bought already roasted, but they cost more than raw nuts and seeds. If you buy raw nuts or seeds, roast or toast them in a low (200 degree) oven, turning from time to time, till tan. If you want ground nut or seed "meal," any blender will do the job in a jiffy.

You can make sandwich or cracker snack spreads:

In the blender, put ½ cup cut carrots, ½ cup pecans, 1 teaspoon corn oil, 1 teaspoon lemon juice, dill. Spread on whole-grain crackers or toast.

The point of this year-long conversion project is *to enjoy more food experiences with the children while withdrawing horrible foods from their eating patterns.* With the children, you can make fun seed and nut edibles:

Crackers: Stir together 1 cup whole-wheat, ¼ cup corn oil, touch of cold water, and salt. When mixture looks doughy, chill it; then roll thin and cut with cookie cutters. Put on oiled cookie sheets. Sprinkle amply with sesame seeds. Toast for 10-15 minutes at 350 degrees; Spread on whole-grain crackers or toast.

Or nut muffins:

In a bowl, put 1 teaspoon baking powder and 1½ cups whole-wheat flour. In the blender, put 1 cup skim milk, 2 eggs, 2 tablespoons oil, 4 tablespoons molasses, ½ cup raisins, ½ cup sesame seeds, ½ cup ground peanuts or pecans, blend. Put all this into the bowl of flour. Drop spoonfuls into oiled muffin or cupcake tin and bake at 350 degrees for 20 minutes.

Or cookies:

Beat 2 egg yolks and add ½ cup honey. Blend in 1 cup ground peanuts or almonds, 6 tablespoons whole-wheat flour and ginger. If you use almonds, change the ginger to almond extract. Fold in the two egg whites, stiffly beaten. Drop from spoon onto oiled cookie sheet, bake at 350 degrees.

With icing:

Blenderize ¼ cup peanut butter, 2 tablespoons oil, ⅓ cup honey, and ¼ cup warm skim milk. Spread on cookies.

Or "healthy" candy (just call it candy, or the appeal will be killed):

Mix together: ½ cup peanut butter, ¼ cup toasted sesame seeds, ½ cup honey, ½ cup regular dry milk powder, ½ cup wheat germ, ¼ cup *finely* chopped apricots, and ½ cup coconut bits. If mixture is too thick, add some liquid skim milk. Roll into small balls, and roll in carob powder (tastes like mild chocolate) or powdered sugar. Chill before serving.

Or luscious holiday desserts:

Walnut torte (or use pecans or almonds): First make the crust: line bottoms of two 8-inch cake pans with foil and brush the foil with 100 percent corn oil margarine. Stir together 1 cup sugar, 3 egg yolks,* 2 cups ground walnuts and ¾ cup wheat germ. Now beat 6 egg whites till stiff and fold into the mixture. Pour the batter into the pans. Bake at 325 degrees for 30 minutes; turn out, and remove paper immediately. Meanwhile, prepare the filling: mix ⅓ cup sugar, ⅓ cup powdered milk, 3 more egg yolks, and ½ cup milk. Stirring constantly, cook until thick but not boiling. Remove from heat, add 1 cup ground walnuts. Spread on cooled layers of torte.

Food events for children's parties:

Popcorn/peanut balls: Boil until brittle when dropped in cold water: 1 cup dark molasses, ½ cup sugar, 1 tablespoon vinegar. Add 1 tablespoon 100 percent corn oil margarine. Pour over 6 cups popcorn and 1 cup salted peanuts; stir. When cool enough to handle, shape into whatever size balls you think suitable.

* Egg yolks are the part of the egg containing cholesterol. When figuring your egg quotient for the week, use techniques such as this: you ate 2 slices of torte, which is about one fourth of it, which is almost a whole egg yolk. The count doesn't have to be compulsively precise unless you're on a physician-prescribed cholesterol diet.

Eat a Variety of Protein Foods

Proteins consist of 20 amino acids. Nutritionists urge us to eat a variety of protein foods because not each protein food contains all 20. By eating a variety of protein foods, without bothering to become a biochemist, the chances are good we'll get all the amino acids— types of protein—that we need.

Devote a Month of the Conversion Plan to:

Examining your recipes and thinking of places to tuck in nuts and seeds.

Important Message to Reluctant Mealmakers

Any time you make a main dish

   stew,
   soup,
   casserole (with fish, cheese, vegetables, or meat),
   patties,
   spreads,
   loaves,

any dish of this type, or any of the grain dishes and baked goods as yet to be discussed, *make twice as much as you'll need so you can freeze the other half for a delicious "heat-and-eat" dinner on a hurried night when you haven't time to "cook."*

What Can Teachers Do?

Perhaps the best way to launch student interest in eating less meat, more *non*-meat protein (fish, poultry, legumes) and more polyunsaturated fat (peanuts, pecans, almonds, vegetable oils and more, again, fish) is to contact the American Heart Association for information about the epidemic of heart disease in this country, and do a health and science unit on heart disease *first*.

There are curriculum materials and plenty of current events treatments of this topic.

Then lead into learning activities regarding *prevention*. What can *we* do, personally, to reduce risk of heart disease later in life? This will lead to information about avoiding smoking and a lifelong low-calorie, low-cholesterol, low-salt diet. Then, you can develop studies and personal projects about smoking and the *application* of all the nutritional concepts in these chapters.

It's at this point that you might suggest a day of the week when the children in your class each bring a lunch featuring interesting nonmeat sandwich fillings, thermos cannister contents, and accessories. If they don't bring lunch, perhaps children could be asked to help at home to see if a nonmeat meal could be prepared once a week. Maybe they could bring a portion for classmates to taste. Or, maybe you could get a cooking corner going. Trail blazer teachers and older students will find a way to work on all this.

Two strong reasons for going at nutrition education this way are 1) to develop student motivation for taking diet seriously and 2) to avoid being in the position of "bossing" students about what they eat. Let them learn the facts from the heart authorities. Then *you* become the *facilitator* to *help* students revise their diets *if they so choose*. Your nutrition education is much more likely to succeed if approached this way than if you simply tell students what to do; for example, not to eat so much meat.

CHAPTER FOURTEEN:

Getting Grain into Kids, or as We Say, Getting Kids into Grain

We've already talked about why grains are good for children. But how does one get grains into them? In the form of:

- Breads, muffins, toast, etc. These foods are frequently popular with children anyway;
- Crackers—already a favorite;
- Cereals—also a staple in most childrens' weekly menu; and pancakes;
- Side dishes, served as we serve potatoes;
- Casseroles;
- Desserts;
- Invisibles—in gravy, sauces, salads, and so on. (We've already tucked a lot of whole-wheat and bran into earlier chapters.)

Lucky Us! Kids Eat These Things As Is!

Children eat all these foods now. All we have to do is slowly, slowly, one step at a time, tactfully, substitute real grain foods for those made of white flour, sugar and chemicals. And gradually introduce new versions of familiar foods: Whole grain foods instead of simulated or stripped grain foods. It isn't necessary to get involved with grinding mills and serious baking unless it appeals. Grains can be gotten into children without going to so much work.

153

Breads, Muffins, Toast, Etc.: Add, Don't Subtract

If the children are used to white bread, the best thing to do is to begin buying other breads as well. Rye, whole-wheat, bran, cornmeal and oatmeal are a few that can always be found in city supermarkets. They're harder to find in the country. But because stores work in terms of demand, if enough people ask for these breads often enough, the stores will soon supply us with them.

What Is Whole Grain?

Without going "on the lecture circuit," a teacher or parent can explain (once, or at most, twice) to children that bread is made from grain. Grain is the seeds of certain grasses which people all over the world grow in fields. Farmers grow these grasses because people eat bread made of the seeds that are part of the grasses. Most of the bread Americans eat is made of one particular kind of grain called wheat. However, there are other kinds of grain from which we make bread: oats, barley, rice, corn, rye and millet.

Before grains can be made into bread, cereal, and so on, they must be separated from the grass, called straw. The grains must also be ground. The wheat berry is the whole grain of wheat. Within the wheat berry is the wheat germ. This is the seedling plant in which lie most of the nutrients grain contains. The coat of the grain of wheat is called bran. Bran is the best roughage we can eat.

When grain is milled and refined to make white flour, the germ and the bran—in other words, the most healthful parts of the grain—are taken out. If grain is ground excessively much, or milled until it is "refined," a great deal of its valuable fiber is lost. Also lost are B vitamins, trace minerals and vitamin E. That's why health specialists urge us to eat whole grain breads rather than refined white breads.

Rye, Whole-Wheat Are Common Breads

If having a sandwich at a lunch counter with the children, be sure to order your sandwich on rye or whole-wheat. You can casually comment that almost all restaurants have these breads because so many people prefer them.

Teachers can encourage children to choose the better breads. Many sandwich "stuffings" (as five year old Felicity calls them) go much better with rye or whole-wheat anyway. The mere fact that parents and teachers are shifting to crisp crunchy buttered rye toast (buttered with 100 percent corn oil margarine, of course) and are eating other such bread, means that many children will soon follow. The tastes and habits of the major adults in a child's life are certainly the single largest influence upon her.

Phase One: Enjoy Don't Withdraw

The strategy here in "phase one" should be to add new breads and allow children to see others enjoying them. Then and only then is it wise to start subtracting the "wrong" breads. Depending upon the degree of dependence on white bread when we begin the transition, and upon the degree of stubborness of each converter, this transition period may last anywhere from a month to six months. Phase one may be viewed as expanding the child's horizons regarding bread by making the unfamiliar familiar.

Focus on the Spread Instead of on the Bread

We want to be giving, generous people. None of us like being stingy and withholding. This means that we'll feel better about what we're doing if we concentrate on producing new cookbooks, new ideas from food magazines, and eliciting new inventions from the children, all aimed at creating a collection of delectable additional spreads and fillings the family likes. Adults who focus on taking white bread away from the kids fail in converting them because they feel guilty and the scene is unpleasant.

During the change over period when we're doing every imaginative, low key thing we can to tempt the kids toward grain breads, it helps to offer a variety of favorite spreads to go with the "funny tasting" breads. These spreads, including jam, may be less desirable than others from a nutrition point of view. Nonetheless, if they help make the switch to grain bread work, they are temporarily "good." Later, they can be shed as the white chemical bread was shed.

Here are a few spreads we can encourage the children to "invent" and experiment with. Provide pretty pots to put them in:

• juice butter
• ground nut butter
• chopped dried fruit butter
• raisin bran butter
• herb butter (carraway, celery and dill seeds are tasty)
• carob butter (tastes like chocolate—some supermarkets and almost all health food stores have carob powder)
• honey butter

Teachers, how about a "bread and butters bar" in the back of your classroom? If available in your stores, or if you have parents who bake, how about serving oatmeal, rice, barley, corn and millet breads, as well as various whole-wheat and cracked wheat breads?

Find Fine New Fillings and Funny Names

Besides transferring each kid's favorite fillings to new breads, study cookbooks and lunch counter menus for new fillings. Encourage informal contests to name each new concoction. Try these:

Garden sandwich: Slice crunchy vegetables (whatever

the children like, whatever you have): cucumbers, green peppers, rutabaga, radishes, carrots or celery, and crunchy bean sprouts; pile any or all of these on mayonnaised or mustarded whole-wheat bread or toast: spread the other piece of bread with blenderized cooked egg plant, broccoli, cauliflower or any other soft vegetable (get rid of leftovers, or use sliced tomato): include a leafy vegetable like lettuce, raw spinach leaves, parsley or cress; add pickles, pepper and other condiments to taste. (Sprinkle in a bit of bran for extra crunch and fiber.)

Yogroom sandwich: ("It isn't a Yogroom sandwich. It's a Mushmato Sandwich.") Spread whole-wheat toast thickly with yogurt; slice on fresh mushrooms, tomato; load up with bean sprouts.

Seed sandwich: Butter rye bread or toast with anything that will glue seeds together, such as margarine, peanut butter, cream cheese, blenderized cooked sweet potato with shredded coconut in it, or any blenderized vegetable; sprinkle thickly with any seeds you like, one or a mixture: carraway, dill, pumpkin, poppy, sesame and so on, plus bran. ("I call it a seedwich," said Sarah. "I make it with lots of sesame seeds and without a top and call it Open Sesame," countered Ted. "I make it with sesame seeds and peanut butter and it's named a Sesame Street," Robbie reports.)

Waldorf sandwich: Stir together equal amounts of chopped apple, chopped celery and walnuts; add mayonnaise to taste; no one will notice a handful of bran if you're interested in our invisible bran idea.

Avaturkey: Mush up a soft avocado; squeeze in ample lemon; spread on well mayonnaised rye toast; cover with sliced turkey and bean sprouts.

Clamwich: Stir together canned minced clams, cottage cheese, and if kids like it, thyme and/or chopped onion; spread and chomp.

Fish wish: Blenderize cooked haddock, halibut, or any

fish you had for dinner last night, with a chopped carrot, a touch of chopped onion or onion salt & bran, dill seeds, and a touch of the child's favorite salad dressing; best on rye toast.

Bread-in-bed: Blenderize or stir together whole-wheat bread crumbs, almonds, bran, and any chopped vegetable the child likes (for moisture). Put the bread crumb mixture "to bed" between two pieces of whole-wheat bread or toast.

Pickle and olive special: There's regular cream cheese and green olive for them as likes 'em; there's dill pickle slices on meatloaf or hamburger, too, all on rye or wholewheat, of course. But for daring folks, Frank invented the Pickle and Olive Special: Spread mustard and ketsup on whole-wheat bread; cover with sliced dill chips and chopped green or black olives; slip in a little bran for extra roughage; blanket with meltable cheese and, if your family likes it, top with chopped onion; broil till sizzley. ("Hee-hee Look at my Pickle-wich!")

Bread Baking As a Way of Winning Children Over to Whole Grain Breads

Even those who don't bake and don't intend to bake might like to bake with the children on two or three weekends while in the transition phase of getting them interested in better breads. Bread wrapped in plastic will keep two to four days, even though it is free of preservatives. We can freez extra loaves and have hot, homemade bread on a busy weekday evening after work. Not only do baked loaves keep for a few days, and frozen loaves keep for a few weeks, even *dough* keeps till the next day or the day after. After mixing the dough, but before letting it rise, we can cover and refrigerate it. If dough is to be refrigerated, double the dose of yease during the mixing process prior to refrigeration. An evening or two later, after dinner while working in the kitchen, we can let another loaf rise and bake for a delicious mid-week breakfast.

Yeast Bread Takes Time; But Its *Own* Time, Not the Parent's

We need not panic at the idea of yeast recipes. Though dough made with yeast does need to sit for an hour or so to rise, and though double rising doughs have to do it twice, busy parents don't sit and twiddle their thumbs while bread rises. We can enjoy activities with the children, go grocery shopping, do office homework, watch TV or whatever we have in mind to do. Bread rises by itself, it does not require our time.

One more thing: always preheat the oven to the recommended temperature before baking.

Even if the bread desn't turn out too well for us amateurs, and even if we aren't ambitions enough to become experts, baking bread with children gets them much more interested in a variety of breads. Encourage the child to stir, taste, knead and sniff throughout.

Whole-wheat: Soften a cake of yeast in ⅓ cup lukewarm skim milk; add 3 tablespoons of molasses. The mixture will rise and bubble. Allow it to do so for 10 minutes. Add 3½ more cups of lukewarm skim milk; ½ cup nutritional yeast, and 10½ cups whole-wheat flour. Mix. Pour this rather runny dough into three oiled loaf pans. Cover them with dish towels. Let the pans sit till the dough has risen nearly to the top of each pan. Bake at 375° for 45 minutes. Isn't the fragrance of baking bread great?

Another whole-wheat bread recipe: Put one package of yeast and ½ cup lukewarm water in mixing bowl. Let sit for five minutes. In a second bowl, put 1 cup skim milk, ½ cup boiling water, and ¼ cup molasses. Mix thoroughly and add yeast water. Now stir in 6 cups whole-wheat flour. Knead well. Let rise for about an hour, or until the dough has doubled in size. Bake at 375° in well oiled loaf pans, or in a tube pan to be fancy. Baking will take 50 minutes.

Double rising rye: This is a very filling bread from my home town, Milwaukee. Boil enough potatoes and water to end up with 2 cups of potatoes and 1 quart of water. Soften 1 cake of yeast in ½ cup lukewarm potato water. Add the rest of the lukewarm potato water and: 2 cups mashed potatoes, ½ cup nutritional yeast, 8 cups rye flour, 4 cups whole-wheat flour, and 1 tablespoon carraway seeds. Blend, knead, oil, cover, leave in bowl in warm spot to rise till double in size. Divide into two balls, oil them again and let them sit on an oiled cookie tin. Each ball will swell to twice its size again! Bake at 375° for an hour.

Spice nut bread: Combine 2 cups whole-wheat flour, 1 tablespoon baking powder, 1 teaspoon cinnamon, ½ teaspoon allspice, ½ teaspoon nutmeg, ⅛ teaspoon cloves and 2 tablespoons of carob powder. Mix well. Separately, cream together 4 tablespoons corn oil margarine, ¾ cup sugar, 1 teaspoon vanilla and 2 beaten eggs. Add one cup applesauce. Stir thoroughly and mix in the dry mixture. Add ½ cup chopped walnuts. Pour or spoon dough into well-oiled loaf pan and bake at 350° for an hour. Always cool bread before taking out of pan and slicing.

Lead bread: (Her children not unkindly call it. It's a term of endearment. Everybody likes this five minute hot, filling bread with a quick supper when parents come home late from work.) Stir together 1¼ cups whole-wheat flour and 3 teaspoons of baking powder. Add 1½ cups all bran cold cereal, 1¼ cups skim milk, 1 egg, and ⅓ cup corn oil. Pour batter into well-oiled muffin pan cups and bake at 400° for 25 minutes, or until muffins are golden brown.

Note: Tell the children that they can make rolls from any bread recipe by making small balls and putting three of them in an oiled muffin pan cup. The balls will merge and swell into a roll. Bake only half as long as you would bake it if bread. Another bit of news the kids will like: any whole-wheat bread recipe will make coffee cake or sweet rolls if you flatten it, cover it with cinnamon, nuts, seeds, raisins, honey, brown sugar, etc., roll it up, and bake it as usual.

Humor and an Aura of Specialness Accelerate Acceptance of Whole Grain Breads

Whenever you can add joking, playfulness and fun to your whole grain bread related conversations you make it easier for the family to swallow the bread and the conversion.

Whenever you bake your own bread or muffins, make serving them a celebration. Use a table cloth, candles, a bread board . . . whatever you can come up with to create an aura of specialness to accompany the delicious aroma of the fresh baked bread. Phychology is the most important ingredient in making food conversion work.

Pumpkin bread: Put together and stir ⅓ cup corn oil, ⅔ cup molasses, ⅔ cup canned puréed pumpkin, 2 beaten eggs, ½ teaspoon each: cinnamon, nutmeg, cloves and ginger. Add 2 tablespoons brewer's yeast, ¼ cup milk powder, 2 cups whole-wheat flour and 1 tablespoon baking powder. Bake at 325 degrees for an hour.

Boston brown bread: Boston brown bread is steamed rather than baked. Mix 1 cup whole-wheat flour, 1 cup rye flour, 1 cup corn meal, and 2 teaspoons baking soda. In another bowl, mix 1¾ cups skim milk, ¾ cup molasses and one cup raisins. Stir wet and dry mixtures together until smooth. Pour batter into two oiled coffee cans, or any round pans you have. Cover tops with foil. Put these cans on a rack in a large pot containing an inch of water. Cover. Steam on top of stove for three hours, replacing water as it steams away. Cool before slicing. This is a good project for a winter weekend afternoon if you are doing housework in and out of the

kitchen anyway. If you make it once, to introduce it to
the kids, you can buy it in cans at the supermarket
from then on.

Corn bread or corn muffins: Blenderize 1 cup buttermilk, 2 eggs, 1 tablespoon oil, ⅛ cup nutritional yeast,
½ cup soy flour, ⅛ cup milk powder, ¾ cup corn
meal. Pour mixture into an oiled baking pan. Bake at
400 degrees for thirty minutes. Pour into well-oiled
muffin tins instead of into bread pans if preferred. To
make corn crunchies instead, pour only a thin layer
into a flat pan, or bake longer. Corn bread is a winner
with most children.

Wheatena muffins: Pour 3 cups Wheatena cereal (lo-
cated with hot cereals in the supermarket) into large
bowl, add 1 cup boiling water. Mix well and let stand.
Add: ½ cup corn oil, 1½ cups sugar, 2 beaten eggs,
2 cups buttermilk. Stir. Then add 2½ cups whole-
wheat flour and 2½ teaspoons baking soda. Mix well.
Fill greased cupcake cups ⅔ full. Bake at 400 degrees
20 minutes or until ready. (The batter for these muffins
may be stored in a covered container for up to two
weeks.) Children seem to like the individuality of
muffins and rolls.

Orange muffins: Soften 1 package dry yeast in ¼ cup
warm orange juice. Warm and then add 1 cup cottage
cheese. Add 3 tablespoons sugar, one teaspoon cinnamon, ½ teaspoon baking soda, 2 tablespoons grated
orange peel or a big spoonful of orange extract and 1
beaten egg. When this has been well mixed add 2 cups
whole-wheat flour slowly. Cover and let sit for several
hours until doubled in bulk. Stir again. Watch the
dough shrink! Put in well-oiled cupcake cups. Cover.
Allow to double in size again. Bake at 350 degrees for
forty-five minutes.

Oatmeal muffins: Stir together one cup whole-wheat
flour, ⅔ cup rolled oats (get in the cereal department
at your store), ⅓ cup soy flour and one teaspoon baking soda. In a separate bowl, combine 1 beaten egg,

1 cup buttermilk or yogurt, 2 tablespoons oil and one tablespoon honey. Mix wet and dry ingredients with as little stirring as possible. Stir in ⅔ cup toasted sunflower seeds or the chopped nuts of your choice. Bake at 400 degrees for twenty-five minutes.

Bran-ana muffins: Stir together 2 cups whole-wheat flour, 1 teaspoon baking powder, and ½ teaspoon baking soda. Separately, stir together 1½ cups mashed, fully ripe banana and 1½ cups all bran cereal. In a third bowl, mix ½ cup corn oil margarine ¾ cup sugar and 2 eggs. Put the three mixtures together, stir well. Add ½ cup chopped nuts. Bake in oiled loaf pan at 350 degrees for an hour.

Stepping Up the Grain Campaign

After several weeks or months of adding new breads to those served and involving the children in trying new spreads and fillings, begin buying less white bread and more other bread each time you're replenishing your supply. Occasionally you might "run out" of white bread. The family will have to make do with what's available. Teachers can suggest to those who purchase food at school that both phase one and phase two above be tried: add new breads, diminish the amount of white bread bought and even, on occasion, "run out" of it.

Higher Expectations: Half and Half

Next, we can start expecting that half the bread each child eats will be grain bread. Confronted with this new state of affairs Jimmy had whole-wheat toast for breakfast and white bread sandwiches in his lunch, "So they won't laugh at me." A month later, his father noticed that he was making a whole-wheat sandwich for school. Daddy said nothing, not wanting to call attention to a desirable situation from which Jimmy might withdraw if confronted with it. The dumbest thing his Dad could of said would have been, "Jimmy, I thought

you didn't like whole-wheat bread!" So Daddy said
nothing. But Jimmy had seen his father notice what he
was doing. He was embarrassed. "The white kind hasn't
any taste," he apologized. Jimmy had discovered that,
unlike store white bread, "real" bread isn't just a container for the sandwich filling; it's a delicious food.

"O.K. Janet," said her Mom. "Let's quit eating white
bread in this house."
Protest.
"O.K., then," negotiated Mom, "I'll tell you what.
I've got a good idea. I'll let you eat white bread each
day for a while yet, if you promise to eat at least as
much other kinds of bread each day. Half your way,
half the healthier way." Janet decided to make each
sandwich with a white top and a grain bread bottom!
It's important that each child is offered as wide a variety of choices and chances for creativity as possible.

Six months after the day she cried because her Mom
said, "Let's quit eating white bread," Janet couldn't
stand it if there was no whole-wheat bread in the bread
box. Once children are off megadoses of junky sweet
foods, it's amazing how they seek the natural sweetness
of whole grain foods.

Whole Grain Crackers for Snackers

Rye Crisp or Seasoned Rye Crisp, a widely available
cracker, is crunchy good, a great base for all sorts of
spreads, cheeses and jellies, and is very nutritious. You
can even make pizza out of it:

Rye Crisp pizza: Spread pizza sauce straight from a jar
to a Rye Crisp. Arrange mozzerella cheese on top. Put
briefly under broiler—till cheese is bubbley.

A quick check of most food stores reveals a variety
of crackers, many of them whole-wheat, corn, rye, rice,
or some other grain. After locating whole grain crackers, see if there are any without food coloring, artificial
flavoring and other chemical additives. If so, you're

doing well, but see if there are some without salt, too.

Many children and teens like crackers and cheeses. Crackers and jam are good, too. Crackers and anything can go to school in lunch bags, and can be eaten for breakfast, after school snacks and before bedtime.

Cereals, a Groovy, Grainy Staple

Most children eat cereal every day. But not everything that goes by the name of cereal *is* primarily *cereal*. Not all "cereal" is nourishing, because not all chief ingredients in cereal boxes are whole grains. Much of what is advertised and eaten as cereal contains more sugar, chemicals and refined grain than whole grain. Often, after bran and wheat germ, the healthiest parts of the wheat, have been taken out, and after what's left has been soaked in sugar, and after chemical color, flavor and preservatives have been added, vitamins are put back in! How sensible it would seem to leave them in in the first place! Children think they're eating cereal, but they're really eating giant chemical encrusted vitamin pills coated with sugar. The only hope is to read labels during several successive shopping trips. Happily, there *are* whole grain, sugar-*less,* relatively chemical-free cold and hot cereals on the supermarket shelves.

One Step at a Time Up to Grainier Eating

During the month the family is converting to whole grains, concentrate for a few weeks on reading bread labels and introducing new breads through buying and baking them, and through the methods suggested above. Then spend a few days or a week thinking about how to shift to whole grain crackers. The time required for the shopper and cook to study each category and sub-category of grain food and to convert shopping and cooking habits is brief, though of course it will take a while longer for everyone to evolve new eating habits and preferences.

Beware of Booby Traps In Brightly Packaged Cereal Boxes

First, look for *whole* grains. Beware of words like "restored" and "enriched." We want real, natural whole grain. Second, look for whole grain (wheat, oats, rye, whatever) *first* on the list of ingredients. First is most. If whole grain is listed in the middle of the list or later, there is only a token amount of it in the box.

Next, watch out for the words "raw sugar," "brown sugar" and "honey." Don't get a raw deal by believing raw sugar or brown sugar is better or less sugary than ordinary sugar. It isn't. Sugar is sugar. Don't get stuck in honey. Honey is just as bad for the teeth and the system as is sugar. Whether it's raw sugar, brown sugar or honey, we'd like to see it near the *end* of the list of ingredients. Last is least.

Third, be aware: If the cereal is some wild, unnatural color, it's dyed; don't buy it. If a fruity flavor is desired, add fruit, don't buy fake fruit flavor. Marshmallow bits are bits of fluffy sugar. And who needs chocolate cereal?

And finally, don't be fooled by words like "sunflower seeds" or "nuts." Even the crunchy granolas can deceive us. Two or three seeds or nuts thrown into a sugary granola cereal doesn't mean much. We can add seeds and nuts and control how much we add. "Wheat germ" is another magic word to watch out for. While it's true that the germ of the wheat is one of the best two parts, it's also true that it can be bought in jars in the cereal department and added to any cereal.

The best bet is probably to buy the whole grain cereals your store carries that contain the least sugar and chemicals. Then add milk, nuts, seeds and the fresh or dry fruits of the childrens' choice. A small amount of wheat germ or bran will add flavor, texture and nutrition.

Besides the better granolas (and only label-reading

will help us know which *are* the better granolas), there are some O.K. cold cereals. Among them are:

Wheaties
Shredded Wheat
Cheerios
Grape Nuts
Kix
Bran Flakes
Special K
Puffed Oats
Corn Flakes
& Life

Kids like their classic morning eye-openers, cold cereals. Great! And continue to let them choose their cereals; but from a pre-selected instead of pre-sweetened collection. Eliminate those that are sugar-frosted, and those with the most additives and those that have been most mercilessly crushed and stripped before identifying a group from which each child can choose. Cold cereal is an excellent after school or bedtime snack, too.

Remember That Day When We Made Granola?

Once (to interest children in new cereals), or more than once, help children make a version of *granola* which can be made without a trip to some exotic health food store:

In a pie pan, at 300 degrees, toast ½ rolled oats and ½ cornmeal. In a bowl, mix half as much wheat germ as the amount of oats you used with chopped or slivered almonds, raisins, pecans or peanuts, sunflower or sesame seeds, chopped dates or apricots, enough corn oil to moisten the mixture, and enough brown sugar or honey to sweeten. Add the toasted grains, stir well, and serve with milk or yogurt.

(As this will keep a while, we can make enough on the weekend to last through the week.)

Something Different for Breakfast

Enjoy a breakfast salad:

In a salad bowl, mix bean sprouts or lettuce (whichever you like or both), sunflower or sesame seeds, chopped apple with peel on, sliced banana, seeded orange or tangerine sections, raisins, coconut, chopped prunes, chopped walnuts or pecans, and as much wheat germ and rolled oats as you can without making your mix too dry. Then add a dressing: either mayonnaise, or yogurt with honey, or vinegar and oil with a little lemon.

This can be made the night before. Or it can be made on a weekend for several weekday breakfasts. With bran muffins, this is quite a super breakfast. (If you baked this quickie recipe last weekend, you'll find some in the freezer right now!)

Another different but perfect dish to serve for breakfast is rice pudding made with brown rice (See MILK chapter for recipe). It contains whole grain (brown rice), milk, raisins and any other dry fruit you put in it, and it's easy . . . just remove from the refrig and serve.

Hot Cereal

Good "store bought" hot grain cereals are Cream of Wheat, Wheatena, Ralston, Oatmeal and cornmeal mush. Many children like cornmeal mush:

Combine ½ cup yellow cornmeal with 2 cups boiling water. Cook and stir over a high flame for a few minutes. When the texture of hot cereal, put in a frying pan with a little corn oil and sauté till crisp. At the same time, sauté sliced apples. Serve together, hot, with molasses, maple syrup or honey.

Wheat germ adds taste and a zesty crunch when added as a topping to hot cereal.

If the children like peanut flavor, the family could occasionally make hot peanut cereal:

To 2½ cups heating skim milk, add ½ cup whole-wheat flour, ¾ cup raw peanut meal, 2 tablespoons of honey, and raisins to taste. Stir, and never let milk boil. Cook slowly, stirring fairly often, for about 15 minutes. (If your store doesn't have peanut meal, but has chopped peanuts, blenderize them and you'll have something quite close to peanut meal.)

Pancakes can be made with whole-wheat flour so the kids gain grain:

Blend 3 eggs, 1½ cups skim milk, 1 tablespoon oil, 1 cup whole-wheat flour, 1 cup soy flour and 3 tablespoons of sugar till the batter is smooth. Pour onto heated oiled pan.

Side Dishes

Rice is a nice "aside" with chicken and many other poultry, meat and fish main dishes. Lamb and rice are a good combination. Brown rice is much more delicious, as well as more nutritious. White rice is white because all the good stuff is taken out of it. Instant rice is worse. If rice is started when we walk in the door from work, it's comfortably done by the time everyone is greeted, the table is set, and the rest of supper has been gotten together. Real rice doesn't take too long for regular working nights.

Boiled and buttered barley is delicious, especially with ham and beef.

Kasha is almost instant quick. It has a stronger taste than rice and makes a marvelous side dish. Serve it with butter, as you would rice. Kasha is coarsely ground buckwheat.

Health food stores sell whole-wheat noodles and whole-wheat spaghetti. If you are one of the few who make your own noodles and spaghetti, use whole-wheat flour instead of white flour.

Grain Main Dishes: Casseroles

Barley stew: Cook 1 cup barley as directed on box
(barley is with rice in the store). At the same time, put
corn oil in a frying pan over a low flame, cut up 2 cups
sliced carrots, 2 stalks chopped celery, 1 sliced onion,
a chopped green pepper and 1 cup sliced mushrooms.
Stir in dill and coriander, or the herbs of your choice.
Or else, use no herbs, but with the barley, cook a ham
bone. Or make barley soup according to the directions
on the package or any recipe you like, but put in less
water; you'll get a good barley stew. Mix the cooked
barley with the vegetables and serve with salad.

Nutty rice: Boil brown rice according to directions on
package. When it's cooked and water-free, add ½ cup
chopped Swiss cheese, ½ cup Parmesan cheese, half
cup walnuts, and a small amount of warm milk. Season
to taste and bake only till cheese melts. Eat while oozy.
Nice with a light salad and a fruit dessert.

We can make all our pasta dishes out of whole grain
spaghetti, noodles or macaroni. If these are unavail-
able, we can add whole-wheat flour to the stuffings and
sauces we use in the recipes involving pastas. Often
bran will fit in, too. All Italian recipes are highly nutritious because they combine grain, dairy, vegetable
and sometimes meat or seafood.

Oriental recipes are highly nutritious. Always use
brown rice with them. Like Italian, Chinese and other
oriental recipes combine grain, vegetables, meat and
seafood. They are not dairy dishes, however.

Tacos are a favorite grainy main dish.

To make taco shells *: Put 1 cup whole-wheat flour,
⅓ cup cornmeal and 2 tablespoons of corn oil in a
blender. Add ¼ cup warm water and blenderize. When
the mixture is a texture you can roll into a ball, re-

---

* Taco shells can be bought ready made in many supermarkets.

frigerate it for an hour or more. Then form 10 little balls. Roll each on a lightly floured board. Fry the flat tacos in a slightly oiled frying pan for 2 minutes on each side and fold in half.

To make taco filling: Sauté the following in corn oil: 1½ pounds lean hamburger, 1 chopped onion, garlic, chili powder, chopped parsley, cumin, celery seed, basil, 6 oz. can of tomato paste, 1 cup water till brown.

Fill each taco "sandwich" with the meat mixture. Top with grated or shredded cheese, diced tomato and a leaf of lettuce (all inside the taco shell).

Grain-Containing Desserts

Cookies, pies, puddings and cakes made with whole grains contain sugar and calories, so should be saved for treats, but they have a much better excuse for being in the diet than do baked desserts made with refined flour and chemicals.

It took a week of the shopper/cook's time to concentrate on converting the household to whole grain bread, and another week to convert to whole grain crackers. It took a week to think through the cereal conversion. It really didn't take a week to add whole grain side dishes, rice and pasta to the weekly diet: This is a matter of gradually serving a different version of the same thing till everyone gets used to the grainier, healthier version, or even prefers it.

The same is true of grain desserts:

1) Use your same old recipes, just substitute whole grain flours for refined white flours.
2) When you feel like making a new dessert or baking something special, try one of ours, or something in one of the fine cookbooks suggested at the end of this book.

Two delicious dessert recipes are in the next chapter:
1) Rice pudding has two blessings, brown rice and lots

of milk; 2) Cottage cheese cake does, too. Here are some easy to make and bake whole grain favorites.

Cookies

Oatmeal cookies: Blend ⅓ cup honey, 1 tablespoon oil, and then stir in 2 beaten eggs, ¾ teaspoon lemon extract OR orange extract OR vanilla (not more than one). If desired, also add ½ cup of any, or any mix of: shredded coconut, chopped dates, raisins, or chopped nuts. Add 1½ cups of oatmeal. After the dough has been well stirred, it should be stiff. If it's too runny, add more oatmeal; if too dry, add skim milk. Drop 20 cookies on oily cookie sheet. Bake at 350 degrees for approximately ten minutes.

Pineapple cookies: Blend ¼ cup honey, ½ cup corn oil, 1 beaten egg, and a little less than 1 cup chopped fresh pineapple. Mix well, and add 1 cup raisins, cinnamon, 2½ cups whole-wheat flour, and 1 cup oatmeal. Adjust amounts of fruit and flour to make dough drop consistency. Drop onto well-oiled pan and bake for twenty minutes at 400 degrees.

Spice cookies: ½ cup honey, ½ cup corn oil, 2 cups whole-wheat flour, cinnamon, allspice, nutmeg, cloves and ginger. Adjust dough by adding flour or fruit juice until stiff. Roll on floured board. Cut with cookie cutters. Pat cookies on oiled cookie sheet and bake at 350 degrees for fifteen minutes.

Molasses cookies: Blend ½ cup molasses, ⅓ cup honey, ½ cup oil, 1 egg, ¼ cup skim milk, ¾ cup powdered milk, 1 cup whole-wheat flour, ½ cup wheat germ, spices and nuts to taste, and 1 teaspoon orange or lemon extract. Bake at 350 degrees for 15 minutes on oiled cookie pan.

Apricot bars: With a scissors, cut 1½ cups dried apricots into 1 cup boiling water and simmer till soft. While the apricots simmer, stir 1 cup wheat germ, 1 cup whole-wheat flour, ⅓ cup oil, ¼ cup corn oil margarine and ⅓ cup honey or sugar together. Press most of the mixture into an oiled 9″ x 9″ pan, saving just enough to spread on top of the apricots. Bake this crust for 10 minutes at 350 degrees. While the apricots are still simmering, make the next layer: Stir together ⅔ cup whole-wheat flour, 1 teaspoon baking powder, 2 beaten eggs, ½ cup honey or sugar, 1 teaspoon almond extract, 1 cup chopped walnuts, and the stewed apricots, which should, by now, be mushy. Take the crust from the oven and spread on this mix. Top with remaining crust. Bake at 350 degrees for 25 minutes, cool, cut, eat.

Carob nut bars: (Carob tastes like chocolate, and can be gotten at many city supermarkets and all health food stores.) Stir together ½ cup corn oil, ½ cup honey, 2 eggs, 1 teaspoon vanilla, ⅓ cup carob powder, ⅔ cup whole-wheat flour, ½ cup milk powder, 1 teaspoon baking powder, 1 cup chopped peanuts. Put into oiled 9″ x 9″ baking pan, and bake for 25 minutes at 325 degrees. Cut after cool.

Cookie Secrets

Convert any cookie recipe you now use. For each cup of white flour, use only ¾ cup whole-wheat OR ANY WHOLE GRAIN flour. For each measure of butter, use the same amount of 100 percent corn oil margarine or corn oil. For each measure of white sugar, use only ⅔ as much molasses (or honey, but unlike molasses, it's no better for us than is sugar). You may need more liquid than your recipe calls for when using whole grain flour. If so, add skim milk or fruit juice as needed. You can add 4 or 5 teaspoons of milk powder to any cookie recipe without it harming the recipe.

Pies

As was said in the fruit chapter, fruit pies made with whole-wheat flour are nutritious, delicious desserts. Here is a basic pie crust:

Whole-wheat pie crust: Stir together 1½ cups whole-wheat flour, ½ cup corn oil, 3 tablespoons ice water. Mix thoroughly, divide in half, make two balls, chill for half-an-hour, roll each ball on well-floured board, or between two pieces of wax paper. Fill two 9″ pie pans, bake at 425 degrees for 20 minutes. Fill with a milk pudding, such as vanilla pudding, slice fruit on top (bananas, strawberries, etc.), and serve warm or chilled, whichever the family prefers.

Whole-wheat pie crust (better for fruit pies): Pour ½ cup boiling water over 1 cup oil. Stir 2 cups whole-wheat flour into liquid and stir thoroughly. Divide in half, chill for 30 minutes, roll each ball separately. Lay one into pie pan. Slice any fruit, with peel on (peaches, apples, etc.) or use any berry, into a bowl. Stir in sugar to taste, squeeze and stir in the juice of a lemon, cut in pats of 100 percent corn oil margarine. Scoop into un-cooked pie shell and sprinkle on cinnamon. Lay on other half rolled dough, pinch top and bottom pie crust edges together, bake at 450 degrees for 10 minutes, and at 350 degrees for another half hour. Always put a cookie sheet on the shelf beneath a fruit pie in the oven while baking to catch the drip.

Unbaked pie crust: Blend ½ cup wheat germ, ¾ cup whole-wheat cracker crumbs, ⅓ cup oil and 1 spoon honey. Press into 9″ pie pan, chill, fill, with whatever you want.

Whole Grain Puddings

Berry pudding: Sprinkle ¼ cup any grain flour over 1 quart any berries. Let stand for half-an-hour. Pour 1 quart hot skim milk over 1½ cups whole grain bread crumbs. Add sugar to taste. Add berry mixture. Pour into oiled casserole. Bake at 350 degrees for 45 minutes. Serve warm with vanilla ice cream.

Apple pan dowdy: Core, peel and quarter 6 apples. Put in a heavily oiled pan. Mix ½ cup sour cream, ½ cup sugar, 1 cup yogurt, and spread over apples. Turn apples over and over in the glop. Sprinkle generously with pumpkin pie spices, or with cloves, cinnamon, and nutmeg. Separately, mix 1 cup whole-wheat flour, 1 cup brown sugar, and ¼ lb. melted 100 percent corn oil margarine. Pour latter mixture on apple mixture. Bake an hour and forty-five minutes at 375 degrees.

Super pumpkin pudding: Mix 1½ cups canned pumpkin, ¾ cup sugar, 1 teaspoon cinnamon, ½ teaspoon each ginger and cloves, 2 slightly beaten eggs and 1¾ light cream. Pour into the above unbaked whole-wheat pie shell and bake 1 hour. For the first 15 minutes, set the oven at 425 degrees; then at 350. Stir together into a pudding before serving. Serve with bits of American cheese, nuts and chocolate bits. This is sin city, a "once-in-a-while," but look at the healthy pumpkin and whole grain it contains if one is going to leave the straight and healthy!

Cakes

Any cake that can be made with white flour can be made with whole-wheat flour. Remember the "equivalent" information given earlier in this chapter. In addition, there are some dandy cakes in the recipe books recommended at the end of this book.

Hopefully, eating much of the "flour power" encouraged in this chapter will increase the healthiness of your family.

CHAPTER FIFTEEN:

Milk Drinkers Love Longer!
And Other Dairy Delights

Milk and milk products can't be overemphasized. To our knowledge, very few nutrition specialists advise against milk. These few feel that cows milk is for cows. There are some infants who do not thrive until taken off milk and put on soy or other nonmilk formula. There are always individual allergies, metabolism problems, and so on that provide exceptions to rules. Each individual has his or her own biology in addition to generic human biology.

Nonetheless, an overwhelming number of nutritionists urge that at least one or two cups of skim milk or the equivalent, be consumed daily by adults, adolescents, and children alike. There is some difference of professional opinion about how *much* daily milk drinking is desirable. The predominant view is 3 or 4 glasses a day for children and teenagers; 2 glasses a day or the equivalent for adults. The equivalent may be a portion of yogurt, cottage cheese, etc. There is also a modicum of disagreement as to whether this need be *skim*. Some say regular milk is all right, except for people with cardiac disease. However, the prevailing view is that skim milk offers all the nutrients for which milk is famous, and fewer detriments: cholesterol and calories. Many pediatricians are beginning to recommend skim milk even for children.

Milk and milk products are so highly recommended —really, urged—because they contain large amounts of protein, vitamins A, B$_2$ (riboflavin) and D and, above all, calcium. They promote the growth of healthy bones, teeth, and skin. In spite of the cholesterol in them, milk products are believed to be one of nature's best gifts. Dairy products are one of the few good places to get calcium. Rickets results from too little calcium.

It's generally possible to see that each person gets the equivalent of 2-4 glasses of skim milk a day:

* Directly or by using it to make milk drinks, soups, puddings, sauces;
* By piggybacking it in powdered form into meat and vegetable patties, loaves, and so on, or
* By adding powdered milk to the regular liquid milk that people drink.

Homemakers will not need to spend more than a month thinking about ways to work milk and milk foods into family meals, through it may take eaters more than a month to convert habits.

Instant milk does not mix with hot liquid as well as plain powdered milk. If we plan to sneak milk powder into favorite family foods undetected, we better not leave tell-tale lumps. If it's mixed according to the directions on the box, it won't lump: add only enough water to make a paste and remove lumps before adding and stirring in the rest of the water. Or use a blender. Chill before serving. Powdered milk should be a household staple, because so many opportunities crop up in which the clever cook can work it into one dish or drink or another. Powdered milk keeps best in a tightly sealed, refrigerated cannister.

Milk

To begin with, there's plain old milk. Millions of children love it. (Then there are those who don't.) Many families find it a good idea to keep both regular milk and skim milk in the refrigerator at all times during the first months of conversion. They allow people to choose, while letting them know why skim milk is better: it's better because it's lower in calories and cholesterol, but equal in nutrients. Gradually, 2 percent or 1 percent butterfat milk can be substituted for regular skim milk. Each week, slightly more skim milk, starting with very little, can be poured into the regular, then into the 2 percent, then into the 1 percent milk, until people have become used to the lighter, clearer taste of skim milk.

Milk Drinks

There are all kinds of instant milk drinks. All can be served hot or cold. All can be made with strongly recommended skim milk. All can be made with cheaper dry milk, but for flavor's sake, mix it right and let it chill for four or more hours before pretending it's milk. Many parents *do* pretend that powdered milk is "real" milk. They even keep it in store containers. Powdered milk is a marvelous natural additive. Put a spoonful in each glass of skim milk and in each bowl of milk soup for enrichment.

Molasses milk: Add molasses and vanilla to skim milk till it tastes good. Molasses is nutritious, yet tastes sweet.

Spice milk: One tablespoon honey (more if essential), nutmeg, cinnamon, and a touch of ginger put in skim milk.

Peanut milk: Put several spoonfuls of *smooth* peanut butter, as little molasses, honey or sugar as possible, and skim milk in the blender. Peanut butter is good protein.

Date or fig milk: Add canned fig juice or chopped dates to skim milk. This will probably be sweet enough without honey or sugar. Blenderize. Dates and figs are filled with fruity nutrients.

Mashed peach milk: Guess how to do it.

Coconut milk: Put as much shredded coconut as desired in skim milk, blend, strain to remove pulp. Coconut is high in cholesterol. But that won't be of concern to the average child.

Berry milk: One cup of any kind of berries (the best are crushed raspberries or strawberries; or try concord grapes), 2 cups skim milk, a touch of lemon and mint blenderized makes a healthy taste treat.

Apricot milk: Soak a handful of dried apricots for 15 minutes, or use canned or fresh apricots, put in blender with one cup skim milk; add brown sugar to taste.

Banana milk: Cut the banana into a cup of skim milk in the blender, add honey if desired, blend.

Pineapple milk: Add crushed pineapple and powdered milk to skim milk and blenderize for a true sensation.

These milkshakes made without ice cream compete very well against the soft-drink industry.

Then there's chocolate milk. Chocolate is a no-no because it contains a great deal of cholesterol and comes imbedded with sugar. It is also high in calories, can rot teeth, and do all the rest of the naughty things sugar does. In addition to sugar, calories, and cholesterol, chocolate contains caffeine, a stimulant to the central nervous system that can "hype up" children till their behavior is impossible.* If children aren't already crazy about chocolate, there is certainly no need to introduce it! If your child, or one of your children, is already a chocolate freak, discuss with him the reasons why you're going to discontinue heavy chocolate consumption. Help him make a list of things he eats that have chocolate in them. Help him reduce his chocolate consumption some each month, focusing on it especially, of course, when "eating-less-sugar" month comes around in his personal conversion schedule. If your child is already a chocolate craver, can you keep chocolate milk down to twice, and later once, a week? The

* And as if this wasn't enough, chocolate is high in sodium (salt), also a no-no.

same goes for cocoa. Can it be saved for a specially frosty moment?

Some children like buttermilk.* Buttermilk *looks* fatty, but is really a low calorie, high nutrient beverage. Buttermilk is best when served *apart* from sweets—it clashes with the sweet taste. It goes especially well with popcorn or cheese and crackers. See if the kids like these nifty buttermilk drinks:

Put ½ cup pineapple juice, ½ cup grape juice, and 1 cup buttermilk in blender and give it the works. Serve over ice.

Buzz in blender 1 cup buttermilk with lemon juice and honey to taste.

Eggnog does contain controversial eggs, but if this can be the way two of the week's egg ration are consumed, the children are in for a treat. Is it a holiday? Does something deserve celebrating? Two egg yolks, 1 cup skim milk, vanilla, with nutmeg and sugar to taste, shaken or blended, will do the trick.

All milk drinks can:

- Be made and go down quickly on busy mornings. In fact, any child of 6 or 7 on up should have no difficulty making them.
- Go hot or cold, depending upon the weather, to school in a thermos.
- Be made the night before by working parents; be put in sealed containers (such as jars), and labeled; be placed prominently in front-row positions in the refrigerator; and be shaken, poured and gulped as an after-school refresher for a hurrying child.
- Be served as the dinner beverage.
- Be swallowed with nutritious nibbles during the evening or at bedtime.

Why fight it? Ride with the tide. Three meals a day are no longer the way. We can try, but snacking seems

* Buttermilk is banned from salt free diets, but is O.K. for a general low salt regimes.

here to stay. Fun foods are the name of the game. But pleasant fun foods need not be nutritionally deficient, nor need a pattern of snacking be unhealthy.

A Hint for Horrified Parents

It's easier to change the snack than the habit.

Note to Coffee Drinkers

Powdered coffee creamers are made of coconut. Thus, they are very high in cholesterol. Most are high in chemicals, as well. If we pick up a half pint of skim milk en route to work and use it instead, we've killed two birds with one stone: avoiding no-nos and drinking milk.

Cereal and Milk

The greatest amount of milk many children "drink" is on cereal. If your children are not drinkers but love cold cereal and use milk with it, offer cereal more often. (See chapter on whole grains for information about cereal.) Milk and cereal are nice after school, in the evening, as supper dessert, and even in a lunch box (but send the packet or baggie of cereal separately, and let the child pour the milk from her ½ pint carton). Most Americans don't eat enough whole grains anyway. Here's your chance to increase the child's milk and grain intake.

Yogurt

Yogurt is increasingly popular and available in this country, and well it should be. Yogurt comes plain and in nearly every conceivable flavor. It's ideal for parents who don't like to cook; children can simply pop the top, pop a spoon in the single serving-size carton, and pop it into the mouth. Babies brought up on it love cool, creamy yogurt. Children enjoy it for breakfast, lunch, snacks, and dinner dessert. Teenagers and adults love it because it has all the value of skim milk yet is not high in calories. Of course, all food contains calories. The idea is to get more nourishment for fewer calories. In this respect, yogurt fills the bill. Yogurt can be bought with or without preservatives. Read labels, buy brands *without*.

Have your children ever made yogurt popsicles? Let them stir brown sugar and cinnamon into plain yogurt, pour it into paper cups with tongue depressors sticking up in the center, and freeze. Or use any flavor yogurt as is.

Milk Soups

Milk soups can also be: consumed for breakfast, put in a lunch thermos cannister, an after-school treat, part of supper, or a before bedtime soother. Many canned soup favorites are milk soups. We can start using *skim* milk in them: cream of chicken, cream of mushrooms, cream of tomato, cream of asparagus, cream of corn, and all the others.

These are two lovely milk soups:

Cream of curried chicken soup: Use leftover chicken, roll in whole wheat flour and sauté in vegetable oil with chopped carrot, onion and lots of mushrooms. Add 2 percent milk, pepper, and curry if you like it. Put through blender, or strain, or eat with pulp.

Cream of vegetable soup: First, cut, sauté and blenderize these fresh or leftover vegetables or those you like: carrots, celery, spinach, corn, onions, lima beans, parsley, etc. Then, add this vegetable purée to *warm* skim milk, pepper, and Worcestershire sauce (the proportions should be 2 cups vegetable purée to 4 cups milk). Do not let the milk boil, though it may get quite hot. Boiled milk is, to quote the young, "yucky."

Cottage Cheese

Cottage cheese, plain on the plate next to the meat and vegetable, is a nice part of dinner. Cottage cheese in the center of a fruit salad is a well-know accompaniment to lunch or dinner. A portion of plain or herbed cottage cheese can go to school in a thermos cannister. Among young children, cottage cheese with milk and sugar is a favorite dessert. Older folks like it too.

Some delicious nonmeat dinner dishes feature cottage cheese. For example:

Baked manicotti: Boil manicotti (a type of pasta found on the shelf next to spaghetti) as instructed by directions on the package. When soft but still firm, drain and stuff with this mixture: cottage cheese flavored with chopped parsley, mozzarella cheese and pepper. Arrange bundles in oiled baking dish with canned spaghetti sauce beneath it and on top of it. Bake at 350 degrees for 15 minutes. Cover with mozzarella cheese and bake 10 more minutes.

For a cottage cheese dish that's rich but extremely nutritious, make and bake:

Cottage cheese cake: Make or buy a graham cracker, granola, or whole-wheat pie crust. Whip 4 eggs in the blender, add 2 cups of cottage cheese a little at a time, blending till smooth. Pour out and add ½ cup honey and 1 teaspoon vanilla. Put into partially baked pie crust, sprinkle with cinnamon and bake for 25 minutes at 350 degrees. Make topping and pour over cake for another 10 minutes of baking: 1½ cups yogurt, 2 teaspoons honey, vanilla. Chill before serving.

And a more sensible but very nice dessert:

Spiced cottage cheese: Mix together cottage cheese, raisins, orange extract, cinnamon, nutmeg, and honey. Pile into fancy dishes or glasses, and garnish with whole or chopped nuts of any kind.

Cheese

All cheeses are highly nutritious dairy products, bearing all the health benefits dairy products bring. But we've discussed cheese before.

Milk Puddings for Dessert

Quick custard: Stir together ½ cup sugar, 1 cup powdered milk. Stir until smooth 4 cups skim milk, 4 eggs, and vanilla. Cook slowly, stirring constantly (about 5 minutes). Chill before serving (serve alone or as a sauce for fruit). For variety, sometimes add peanut butter or shredded coconut, and honey instead of sugar.

Rice pudding: Use leftover cooked brown rice. Stir in honey; add one, any or all of the following: chopped walnuts, pecans, cut-up mandarin oranges and canned apricots, dates and canned pineapple, coconut shreds, raisins, sweetened wheat germ, cinnamon, nutmeg, and ginger. Put in well-oiled baking dish mixed or in layers and bake at 350 degrees for ½ hour.

Milk-and-fruit whip (tastes like sherbet): Chill 1 cup evaporated milk in ice tray till it starts crystallizing and then whip it (it won't whip until it's very cold). Add 8 tablespoons lemon juice (takes away the evaporated milk taste), 8 tablespoons of sugar (oh, well, it's dessert, after all), 8 tablespoons of powdered milk (for enrichment), and vanilla. Stir in 4 cups of mashed or puréed fruit. Serve cold.

Honey-almond milk pudding: Unflavored gelatin comes in small packets, and is not a no-no like jello. *Unflavored gelatin* does not contain artificial flavors and colors. For this special occasion dessert delight, soften the contents of a packet of gelatin in ½ cup cold milk. Put 1½ more cups of milk and 2 egg yolks in top of double boiler and stir slowly until mixture thickens. Remove from heat. In shallow pan, combine mixture

with dissolved gelatin. Add 2 beaten egg whites, 4 tablespoons honey, and almond extract. Chill until firm after
sprinkling with slivered almonds.

Milk Jello: Add ½ cup boiling water to one packet
unflavored gelatin. When dissolved add 2 cups skim
milk & cinnamon to taste. Let set in refrigerator.

Questions About Prepared Whipped Toppings

Read labels. Is this *milk? Skim* milk? Are there
chemicals in this? What *is* this, anyway? Couldn't we
skip it?

Homemade Ice Milk

Ice cream *with no artificial flavors and colors* is
available in many supermarkets. Read labels and buy a
"safe" brand, if you must buy it at all. Ice milk is also
available. Though it has the calories and cholesterol of
whole milk and contains sugar, it has far fewer calories
and also has less cholesterol than ice cream. It's cream
contrasted with milk. Ice cream is one of the least desirable dairy products as far as nutrition goes. It does
not have the nutrients milk does, but does have more
saturated fat (the type to avoid). On the other hand,
as rich desserts go, it's not the worst.

For every day, ice milk is recommended. Ice cream
is okay once in a while.

Milkshakes: Enrich 1 cup skim milk with a spoonful of
powdered milk, and add 1 scoop any flavor ice milk (if
it's vanilla, add vanilla). Or leave out the ice milk,
and put in sweetened evaporated milk instead. (Evaporated milk contains *twice* the nutrients of milk in *half*
the liquid.) If you add malt, you add calories, but also
a yummy flavor. A can of malt is easy to keep on hand.

Best of all, for fun and flavor, does your family *make*
ice milk? Busy parents, you can stay busy; don't fuss.
The children, if they're over 8, can do it. It's made in

an ice tray in the freezer of any refrigerator. Freeze at the lowest temperature on the dial and beat twice during the freezing process to make the ice milk light and fluffy.

Any-berry ice milk: (You can also use any puréed fresh or canned fruit.) For example, stir together 4 cups milk, 2 cups canned or fresh raspberries (or strawberries or peaches) that have been blenderized, 2 cups granulated sugar; freeze to mushy consistency. Beat. Freeze to firm; eat. (If you use pineapple, use canned crushed. Fresh pineapple will keep the mixture from freezing.)

Any-juice milk sherbet (another term for ice milk): For instance, combine 2½ cups grape juice, ¾ cup granulated sugar, and 4 cups milk. Blenderize to make frothy. Freeze to mushy consistency. Beat. Freeze to firm.

Molding ice milk or sherbets (see chapter on fruit) is simple, but these desserts astound everyone, especially children, with their glamour. When the freezing mixture is quite far along the way but still pliable, push and pack it into every crevice and corner of the *prechilled* mold you've chosen—which can be any jello mold, bowl, or interesting tin can. Cover with foil and freeze for at least 4 hours. When ready to serve, place a plate on the open side of the mold, and hold it briefly upside down under hot water. The ice milk will fall neatly out. If necessary, wipe the mold with a hot, wet dish towel, or insert a knife at one point only to release the air holding the frozen form. A perfect idea for birthday parties.

What Can Teachers Do to Promote Dairy Products?

Teachers can interest children, teenagers and young adults in discarding their colas and other soft drinks and in moving to the softest drink of all—nature's own sweet milk. Next time a young person is drinking or discussing soft drinks, throw out a few facts. For example, tell her that soft drinks have no nutrients, yet fill the belly where a nutritious beverage belongs. This deprives the drinker of nourishment she needs. Make jokes about your "deprived" children. Tell them they're "disadvantaging" themselves.

Get the class into a conversation, on the spur of the moment or later in the week, about things to drink other than soft drinks. As students mention Kool-Aide and phony fruit "drinks," suggest that they read labels, next time it's convenient. Then they'll know just what it is they're drinking when they swig these fake drinks (sugar, artificial colors, artificial flavors, and caffeine in colas and in Dr. Pepper, as well as *very* expensive water!). During the week, as members of the class bring up their findings, discuss the fact that nutritionists worry about Americans' mad rate of sugar consumption (see the sugar chapter later in this book). Discuss the fact that cancer specialists worry about Americans' mad rate of chemical consumption. Ask what else there is to drink. When they suggest alcohol, tea, and coffee, tell them about the negative aspects of these, too.

Any time a legitimate beverage is mentioned—milk, fruit or vegetable beverage—clap, smile, indicate delight, make the idea of drinking it fun. Start listing nourishing drinks big and bold on a chart that all can see. The more the merrier, even if charts are hanging everywhere.

After a few weeks of this casual approach (grim intensity on this topic turns people off), suggest that one day of the week be "Drink Milk Day." Encourage children to experiment at home. Let them invent drinks such as those described earlier in this chapter. Regardless of what level of specialized subject you teach, it isn't impossible for class members to bring a milk drink in a thermos once a week, or at least a recipe, which can be written on the chalkboard and copied by other students. The fringe benefit here is that families may become more aware of diet. In some situations, it's possible to set up a table and ingredients, where once a week people can mix the "milk drink of the week." *

If students become interested in concocting fruit or vegetable drinks too, encourage them to branch out along those lines. In addition, try to create interest in other dairy products. At an opportune moment, get kids talking about other dairy products they can think of: cheese, soup, yogurt, cottage cheese, pudding, etc.

As the weeks go by, suggest that students make some of these foods at home and bring them to weekly tasting parties. In fact this can be a regular "dish-a-week" homework assignment. If circumstances permit, prepare one dairy dish a week right in the classroom.

Now's the time for the class to make a cookbook containing all your dairy delights to date, and any fruit and vegetable bonuses that have been introduced. Each person can help write, duplicate, illustrate or whatever. The book can be sold inexpensively to students and parents in the community.

At this point, why not help the children start a dairy bar for the school? Depending on the age of the youngsters, this can be a more or less elaborate project. At any rate, it will involve nutrition education, language arts, math, community spirit, and much more.

When everyone's involved to this extent, it should be relatively easy to expand the project to other food categories. You can get films or film strips, take field trips, make up funny lyrics about food for songs, encourage independent reading, create posters and dramatizations. All the usual methods of presenting curriculum can be applied to health-giving foods. Who knows, *your* class may even be the group that gets the soft drink machine banished from school premises.

---

* Need it be said? A child may be under doctor's orders not to ingest *any* of the many food categories discussed in this book. Teachers should alway be matter-of-fact about children who are exceptional in any way. They should teach tolerance, and should include the "different" child as suitable.

CHAPTER SIXTEEN:

Many Americans Eat Five-to-Twenty Times Too Much Salt

It's estimated by experts that many Americans eat five-to-twenty times more than their daily requirement of salt. Diet, and particularly salt, are related to hypertension.

Hypertension, a Major Killer

Hypertension is the greatest single cause of death in this country. More than 24 million Americans have it. It causes 60,000 Americans a year to die. Many people don't even know they have it, because they don't have physical examinations at regular intervals. According to hypertension authorities such as Lawrence Galton, to no small extent, strokes, heart disease, kidney failure, loss of vision, and other serious problems represent the *complications* of hypertension. They are, in effect, *results* of uncontrolled high blood pressure.

High blood pressure is twice as common in the children of hypertensive parents—or a parent who was not *known* to be hypertensive, but who died of or suffered stroke, heart disease or kidney disease, all of which may be manifestations of high blood pressure.

Stress and Hypertension

That stressful situations and strong emotions can cause blood pressure elevations has been well documented. When a person is angry or afraid, his or her blood pressure may go up. Some people react to even mild life stresses with rise in blood pressure. The Amer-

ican Heart Association says that bodies that get used
to responding to daily life as if it were a series of
emergencies, often develop hypertension. People who
bottle up their anger are better candidates for hypertension than are those who express anger, or better yet,
those who don't have cause to *be* so angry. Many
noted experts believe that the clue to the cause of
hypertension lies in the interpersonal "games people
play."

Causes and Cures

The fact is that at the moment, medical science
doesn't *know* the cause of 90 percent of diagnosed
cases of hypertension. Yet virtually every single case of
hypertension—from the mildest to the most severe,
Dr. Galton and other specialists tell us—can now be
treated effectively. Though there are known causes and
cures for only ten percent of the hypertension cases,
all other kinds can be controlled through exercise, giving up smoking, drugs, *reducing diets, and salt-free
diets*.

Prevention and Hypertension

Hypertension is one of the most neglected of all
major health problems. Specialists recommend that
where there's a family history of hypertension, parents
should help their children avoid possible precipitating
factors, by minimizing emotional stress, treating kidney
infections, *guiding children in keeping their weight
down, and limiting salt intake*.

Salt and Hypertension

Another highly respected authority on hypertension,
Lewis K. Dahl, M.D., says the evidence that salt in-
duces permanent and fatal hypertension in rats is direct,
quantitative and unequivocal. However, considering
that the extensive evidence regarding the relation-

ship of salt and hypertension in people is circumstantial, and because hypertension, along with the other most prevalent cardiovascular disease atherosclerosis, *is generated in the earliest years of life, not five decades later when diagnosed,* people, pediatricians, parents, and physicians in general, don't pay attention to limiting salt intake throughout life.

Scientists specializing in salt and the human body say that there is popular misunderstanding about the need for salt. Historically, there have apparently been people living throughout the world, in the artic, desert, jungle, and plains, who went for centuries without salt other than that contained naturally in food. Actual metabolic requirements for sodium (salt) in the average person are remarkably small.

It's hard to see how it could be actively *good* for children to eat food canned and cooked with salt, and salted at the table, and then to snack on heavily salted crackers, potato chips, nuts, popcorn, pretzels, and high sodium commercial baked goods, etc. throughout the day.

Converting to a Low Salt Diet

Without putting the family and the children on a salt free diet, which is very stringent, unpleasant and needn't be done unless the doctor says so, it's possible to *lower* daily salt consumption, and move to a *low* salt diet.

Another word for salt is sodium. Sodium is found naturally in all foods. Fruits and vegetables, in general, have little sodium unless it's added in canning. Because sodium is frequently added in canning and in prepared foods, fresh fruits and vegetables are safest. We've said this all along anyway, even without reference to salt. Much more sodium is found naturally in high protein foods such as meat, eggs, cheese and milk. This is all the more reason not to eat much meat, eggs, and cheese, and not to go overboard on milk. The worst meats for sodium are dried, salted, smoked or canned meats, and are on our *eat less* or, better yet, *eat none* list *anyway:* bacon, ham, sausage, bologna, and salami. Fish preserved with salt should be avoided too: smoked fish, anchovies, and sardines. Clams, crabs, lobsters, oysters, scallops and shrimp are moderately high in sodium, and we already have *dis*recommended them because of cholesterol.

For those wishing to eat less salt, here are a few simple suggestions:

- Use no salt in the preparation of foods (people probably won't know the difference, don't mention it).*
- Don't keep salt on the table (tell people why—or wean them more slowly, encouraging each salter to use salt only on the foods where it matters most).
- Avoid all excessively salty snack foods.
- Follow basic principles given earlier in this guidebook.

Doing the above will make a lot of difference in daily salt intake, but for people seeking tighter control:

- Read labels on all commercially prepared foods, and avoid those that list sodium or soda compounds.
- Avoid bouillon, ketsup, chili sauce, pickles, relishes, canned, frozen, and powdered soups, Worcestershire and soy sauce, and other meat sauces, which are made with lots of sodium.
- Don't use baking soda or foods containing it.

Most regular crackers, cakes, cookies, ice cream, sherbert, pastry, prepared mixes, jello, biscuits, and commercial chocolate in various forms (syrup, bars, etc.) are high in sodium and should be avoided, but these foods we've already talked about in the context of grain, milk, and *sugar*.

Teachers can help a lot by teaching the above realities, and by banning salted junk foods.

* You may have noticed that almost all recipes in this book are salt free. Now you know why!

For many, eating less salt is one of the easiest parts of the conversion project, because so much of the salt we consume is hidden. As we don't know we eat it anyway, it can be eliminated without aggravation.

The hardest thing for salt addicts to stop, is "snowing" their food at the table. Until the salt taste is extremely acute, they find that food tastes bland and meaningless. They'd rather not eat it. Weaning oneself away from salt *gradually* works best. Some salt freaks require *several* months to convert salt-wise. A squeeze of lemon wherever a slug of salt would've gone improves saltlessness immensely. But real salvation lies in the fact that the duller the food tastes, the less one eats of it, and most Americans would do well to eat less anyway.

This SALT chapter is a short chapter, but for many people shifting from excessive salt consumption to modest salt consumption will not be "a short chapter." Eating less salt is easier said than done, but we can do it.

CHAPTER SEVENTEEN:

Many Americans Eat 102 Pounds of Added Sugar a Year

What can one say about this heavy sugar habit? If, upon reflection, parents and teachers decide that 102 pounds of sugar *beyond* that which is already put by nature into fruit, grain, milk, and so on, doesn't harm their children's long range health, they'll let them eat it. They will (if this situation doesn't seem dangerous to them), allow their children to consume an additional 24 lbs. of corn syrup and other sweeteners. It's estimated that for some children sugar makes up approximately 20 percent of the daily diet!

Parents, teachers, and others in charge of children who consider this constant wash of sugar flowing through their children's bloodstreams and drilling at their teeth O.K., will continue to permit it. They will permit it regardless of common sense, the protestations of distressed nutritionists, and the fact that they've fallen victim to the sugar industry's objective rather than remaining on target toward what one might imagine to be their own objective—health—through a diet directed at the development of *maximum* health. These parents may even justify allowing their children to lace their food and spike their drinks with sugar by jerring at common sense, and insisting on "scientific" proof that sugar is bad for bodies. Whether or not such excessive amounts of sugar *are* harmful, will not be the factor determining adult decisions. People do what they *want* to do, whether or not it's wise.

Grownups Don't Want to Seem Mean

Even some parents and teachers who guiltily believe that their children shouldn't consume constant quantities of sugar, syrup, jam, jellies, honey, candy, cookies, pies, cakes, doughnuts, many kinds of crackers, gum, sugar-coated breakfast cereals, soft drinks, jello, puddings, ice cream, etc., will continue to *let* their kids consume these sugar laden nutritional nothings, because they feel "mean" saying no.

Secret Sources of Sugar

Furthermore, adults who don't care about this will ignore the fact that sugar slides into bodies as an invisible added ingredient in all sorts of unlikely food products from canned goods to ketsup. Children of parents who aren't on the alert, will eat unknown quantities. Dextrose means sugar. Carbohydrates may mean sugar, carefully concealed in cagey language. *Glucose* is an essential element in the human body. However, sucrose, refined sugar made from sugar beets and sugar cane, is not an essential element. Honey, brown sugar, and raw sugar, as well as sugar, mean sugar. To the cells of the body, it's all the same.

We've Been Sold a Sweet Bill of Goods

Apparently, children, teachers and the rest of the purchasing public, have, through behavior, convinced advertisers that we'll buy anything, as long as it has either sex appeal or sugar appeal. Alcohol pacifies some people. Tranquilizers and drugs of every type pacify other people. Sugar is the pacifier of many others. TV, probably the greatest sugar pusher in the nation, has effectively addicted many people to the insidious sweet soothings it sells. Sugar has silently and sweetly made its sorry way from where it was early in history (a pinch of this rare and expensive substance was occasionally put into prescriptions by apothecaries), to where it is today: in every mouth, most every hour of the day. Sugar pushing advertising comes strategically slanted toward whatever pitch is currently popular. The only safe response to it is to suspect that whatever is pushed hardest, we need least. If we really need it, we'd know it without so much pressure. We can teach our children to ignore slick and sticky sugar pushing ads.

Naked Calories Prevent Nourishment

According to many noted nutrition authorities, excess sugar consumption is America's #1 nutritional "crime." High sugar consumption automatically spells poor nutrition. This is because sugar provides calories devoid of minerals, amino acids, and vitamins, and at the same time kills appetite, and causes people to spurn foods that do contain these nutrients. Sugar calories are "naked" calories that prevent the eating of nutrients needed by cells.

Sweetened Confusion

It's true that sugar is energy, and bodies need it. But we've been beautifully bamboozled on this subject by the sugar industry. When children eat fruit, they get fructose, the type of sugar that comes in fruit. When children eat foods containing malt, they get maltose, which is malt sugar. When children drink milk, they get lactose; milk sugar. When children eat fruits and vegetables containing other sugars, they usually are getting glucose also. Besides, our bodies convert many of our major foods into glucose. Glucose is always in our blood. Glucose is "blood sugar." Sugar (glucose) is essential to good health. Sugar (sucrose) is thought by many to be extremely bad for our health.

Almost all nutrition specialists, except those whose work is supported by the sugar industry, believe that today's children eat far too much sugar. However, as has already been said, what nutritionists believe won't influence what children eat. What parents and teachers believe, will influence what children eat.

Sugar-Glutted Bodies in a Sugar-Coated Culture

We do not yet know that excess sugar consumption is unrelated to our cancer epidemic. Some cancer specialists suspect a connection. We do not yet know if it's true, as some specialists think, that many undiagnosed people have hypoglycemia, a prediabetic condition, caused by excess sugar consumption. We do not yet know if depression, hyperactivity, and other increasingly common psychiatric problems are related to increasing sugar consumption. We do not have the evidence yet, about sugar and long term health or illness, because previous generations didn't eat sugar in anywhere near the quantities our children do. Do we want our children to be guinea pigs to help future generations find out what happens if one eats 102 pounds or more of sugar per year and goes from cradle to grave in a sugar stupor? Or will we choose the lower risk route—a low sugar diet *pattern,* with occasional sweet treat exceptions?

Adults as Guides

A word of encouragement to timid child carers: Among those of us child development specialists *most* concerned with the nuances of psychosocial development and the creation of free spirits—those of us *least* likely to limit children unnecessarily—are many experts who are advising parents not to stand idly and over permissively by while their children succumb to America's wild and woolly, runaway sugar consumption, and become nymphomaniacs for sweets.

What can be done? Nothing by parents who unconsciously wish to allow harm to befall their children, while not actively harming them. And nothing by weak parents. There's too much flim-flam from advertisers, social pressure from peers and temptation from everywhere for weak parents to resist. But there are some steps that parents who want to can take to achieve a less sugar-drenched upbringing for their children.

Sugar-Freeing the Children

First, we can "run out" of sugar foods, and buy no more without calculatedly intending to. We tend to bring lots of sugar loaded foods into our homes without noticing. Teachers, too, can exclude sugar foods from children's experiences at school.

Second, we can state firmly that we, "along with most people we know," have been bewitched by well crystalized sugar consumption customs, but that now we realize what we've been allowing to happen to our bodies. We're going to cut out this sugar abusive treatment of ourselves. We're going to emancipate ourselves from sugar slavery. We can give children brief information about why we're no longer buying barrels full of sugar foods, and can refuse to be wheedled into relenting.

Thirdly, we can help children feel "in" by explaining to them how politics work. Laws, including pure food and drug laws, are made by legislators in response to pressure they feel. If legislators receive pressure primarily from those who benefit financially from selling something, sugar included, the legislators will make laws representing the seller's intersts. Only when legislators receive more pressure from citizens and consumers wanting something different—in this case, protection from misleading sugar sellers—will laws protecting people be made. In the meantime, as sugar producing, shipping, and selling has proved a source of personal wealth and national importance, we can expect the government not to sound the alarm against it.

Fourthly, we can teach children how addiction

works. Craving something isn't needing it. We can em-
pathize with the child's desire without giving in to it.
The exact same concepts and terminology can be used
in explaining sugar addiction to children as those we
use in explaining drug abuse. If we frequently comment
upon our confidence in the child's ability to control his
impulse to do as the other children are doing and to
satisfy his yearning for sweet drinks and snacks, we
build his own capacity for impulse control.

Fifth, we can help each child decide when he or she
really truly wants a special treat (sweet), and which
one. Sweets are consumed far less frequently this way,
and are enjoyed much more. Some children will discontinue eating baked goods, if they can continue to eat
ice cream once in a while. Other children will graciously give up commercial candy, if they can still
bake and eat cookies from time to time. To each his
own should be a governing principle, while kicking the
habit of constant, almost unnoticed sweet eating.

Sixth, if we teach children about "sweet and dangerous," and help them become involved in the entire
conversion project, we build their own capacity for
leading others. We can help them do so, in ways that
are modest, not "weird," and not likely to alienate
them from their sugary, self-saturating friends.

After a few weeks of all the steps above, plus the
introduction of happy new fruit and other food treats
as suggested in earlier chapters, we can commence a
policy of punishing yammers for sweets. For example,
parents could say, "If you clamour for sweets urged by
TV, you can't watch TV." Parents are not required by
law to let their impressionable children be the captive
customers of the insidious peddlers of sweets. "If you
fuss for sweet junk foods in the grocery store, you can't
come along when I go there." Instead offer the child a
choice of healthy treats to eat when you shop.

Children expect grownups to guide them. If we set a
good example, serve many new delicious drinks and
foods, gradually withdraw sweets, and teach children to

avoid temptation, they will, on the whole, comply. Children feel well cared for if we explain that most people's bodies can't handle such sugar excesses and that we don't want them to die trying. If we are affectionately firm in our sugarless policy, the average child will go along with us.

CHAPTER EIGHTEEN:

Many Americans Eat ? Pounds of Chemicals a Year

It's a fact that over 2,800 chemicals are added to the ordinary foods we eat. It's a fact that very little research has been done on the effect these chemicals have on the human body. It's a fact that no research has been done on me and my children or you and yours as to which combinations of chemicals in what quantities are consumed in a day, by any specific individual. We eat chemicals for breakfast. We eat chemicals for lunch. We eat chemicals for dinner. We eat chemicals between meals. And all collect in the same gathering ground, the stomach. It's a fact that all food consists of chemicals, but it's also a fact that nature is a brilliant balance, and when we tamper with it we need to study the consequences before assuming they're harmless.

Of Predators and Profiteers

Though food industry magnates and managers are doubtless not the malevolent monsters that apoplectic ally angry food faddists accuse them of being, grimly grinning and counting their gold as we gulp cancer-producing chemicals, they aren't helpful to the nation's nutritional needs, either. Though images of these corporate criminals slyly slipping cancer causing (carcinogenic) foods into all the corners of our cupboards are, to say the least, peculiarly distorted, the hand-in-hand politics and economics of the food industry and the federal government do not promote consumer protection.

But there is much silliness and some quackery in every field, and thanks to misleading advertising, most

Americans are nutritional ignoramuses and myth riddled eaters. Some food facts are distributed via mass media. But how to sort out the truth and resist the magical twaddle and thundering work of the counter offensive constantly coming across the TV screen, we would dearly like to know. Over any common food sense that's sent our way, careen the media's myths, founded on fears, fantasies, and America's impulsive need for instant happiness via romatic chemical tonics and the pervasive persuasion of admen, who counsel us majestically from the air.

Children can be taught to smile knowingly at the clangor of the admen's style. They can learn to see the humor as these fellows rattle and chatter all day long. We can help children develop the capacity to cope with all this nudging and bludgeoning of the mind by developing judgment based on fact.

Though life isn't a simple "fault"/"no fault" matter, there are facts and the chemical facts are these.

The Synthetic Infiltration

In the old days, people grew what they ate, and preserved it as best they could with cold cellars, ice cooling, spices, smoke, and salt. Urbanization meant that many people had no gardens or animals. Food for them had to be hauled long distances. Hence the invention of preservatives. In the mid-nineteenth century, food coloring was invented. By 1900, approximately eighty dyes made from coal-tar oil were put in American edibles. In 1906, a Food and Drug Act came into being, and the majority of these food colorings were banned. Since then, artificial colorings have again proliferated. Research indicates that coal-tar compounds, from which dyes are made, have either carcinogenic or mutagenic characteristics. Society understandably frowns upon using people as lab specimens upon which to test cancer and mutation causing chemicals. Therefore, most of what we know, we know from what happens to animals in response to these chemicals. The human being is an animal, and is not exempt from allergy, illness and death. Until more research has been done, it's a fact that we can't know whether or not we're safe from the carcinogens known to exist in food coloring.

Food flavoring—synthetic taste, copied by chemists from *real* flavors—also infiltrates much of our food. It's estimated that nearly 1,500 fake flavors infest our food.

In 1965, 2,764 intentional additives were known by the Academy of Sciences to be in use in food. In 1971, there were 3,800. At this rate of increase, food itself will soon not fit in the containers, and we can eat pure chemicals. Food colors and flavors run a phantasmagoric gamut to persuade the purchaser. Their persuasiveness shows in the shopping cart. Their hazards may show in the soaring cancer rate.

It's a fact that no previous generation anywhere in the world has ever consumed chemical additives in this quantity. We have no historical experience of safety on which to base a feeling of security as we swallow these unnatural multisyllabic substances. We are filled and fooled with food "fortifications," and "enrichments" rather than food. More and more, instead of adding a few extra nutrients to wholesome food, manufacturers are stirring a few food ingredients into a pot of chemicals.

It's a fact that until the early 1970's the National Cancer Institute wasn't focusing on research concerning the relationship of nutrition and diet to cancer. Until the Candle Lighters, a group of parents whose children have or have died of cancer, put pressure on NCI, this wasn't a major concern. Even now, experts there say that the number of chemicals researchers would have to contend with are astronomical, plus complicated factors such as the effect of *other* foods (fiber, for example) on the chemicals, of fecal flora, of transit time through the colon, etc., are overwhelming, and it will be many years before they know significant facts about toxicity of chemicals in food in connection with cancer.

*After considering all these facts, it's common sense
to think that we should, whenever conveniently possible, avoid food and drink containing chemicals until
research has conclusively proven each and every one,
in every combination and quantity, in every human
body to be noncarcinogenic—in other words, to be
safe.*

Perhaps it's archaically conservative, but it's a fact
that some people, including some pediatricians and
other physicians, believe it unwise to bomb bodies with
chemicals from infancy onward.

Squinting Through the Printing

We bypass a great many chemicals if we read labels
and avoid buying foods that list artificial flavoring,
artificial colorings, BHA, BHT, nitrites, and nitrates.
If in addition we attempt to buy brands that do *not*
contain other preservatives, softeners, flavor intensi-
fiers, modifiers, potentiators, and nonnatural ingredients in general, we bypass many more chemicals. It's
hard to tiptoe through the grocery store minefield
wending our way cautiously through the clauses, small
print, and jargon behind which the profit-oriented food
industry hides, but it can be done. It would be easier to
shop sanely if the law required labels to list *specifics,*
in average size type, banned misleading wordage, and
insisted that ingredients be prominently named, rather
than murmured in miniprint, blending through a bleed-
off into a bottle-cap crimp.

At present, manufacturers of many categories of
foods *aren't even required to list the ingredients on the
labels of their products,* so even well-trained, scrupu-
lous, label-reading shoppers can't know what they want
to know. Concerned consumers can campaign for laws
forcing all ingredients in every food to be named. Another problem in label-reading is to be onto tricks of
the trade: *imitation* corn is *not* corn; *chocolately* is *not*
chocolate; *tastes like real meat* is *not* real meat; *buttery*
or *artificial butter flavor isn't* butter; and so on. Per-

haps any food with an imitation texture, color, flavor, etc., should be required to say "not real food."

Surely we can rest assured that the reason the food industry adds artificial flavors, colors, and textures is to cover up cosmetically for the fact that it can then remove genuine flavors, colors, and textures by using inferior or substitute foods and primp them up to look like what we thought we were buying. We can gorge fattening amounts of fake foods and be getting extremely poor nutrition.

Governmental Protection From Poisons

Some people think the government should protect innocent eaters, who do not wish to learn the lingo of chemists in order to make it safely through the supermarket. Others consider this an invasion of their freedom. They feel they should be free to eat ground glass if they want to.

We can't assume that because the food industry and the government give us 3,800 chemical additives they're safe. Many top positions in the Food and Drug Administration are filled with folks who have formerly been executives in the food industry. Few key people in FDA have come from consumer groups. Scientists are not error free, or exempt from the political pressures of their times. Scientific kowtowing to industry, politics and pocketbooks isn't unheard of. Many a medical misadventure has had its effects on everyday people's lives. And the medical pendulum swings—what's incontrovertable scientific fact to one generation is poppycock to the next. We all want to be free. But many a perceived freedom, results in impaling us upon someone else's financial advantage.

A Fantasy: Modern Day Christmas at Grandmother's House

We realize how heavily synthetics have penetrated our food supply when in 1978 we contemplate going to

Grandmother's house for our traditional Christmas dinner.

Our Gramma is no teetotaler, so we start with cocktails. The drink is made of pussycat mix with citric acid, corn syrup solids, gum arabic, sodium citrate, calcium phosphate, artificial color and BHA. There are h'or d'oeuvres. We have slices of salami (with dextrose, lactic acid starter culture and sodium nitrite), and cute little pizza canapes (containing calcium propionate, L-cysteine, hydrolized vegetable protein, imitation mozzarella cheese, calcium caseinate, disodium phosphate, emulsified, stabilizer, artificial flavor, a pasteurized processed cheese product, sodium phosphate, citric acid, artificial color, ascorbic acid, smoked flavorings, sodium nitrate, sodium nitrite, sodium glutamate, and real honest-to-God green peppers).

The soup is dull, having only five chemicals in it, but Gramma adds pre-made croutons, and these liven up the broth with monocalcium phosphate, monsodium glutamate, ammonium sulfate, potassium iodate, calcium propionate, BHA and BHT.

The self-basting turkey has been infused with chemicals, which when heated are released, so bathe our bodies with their deliciously poisonous flavors. We enjoy the crisp crunchiness of the pre-prepared vegetables, with their varying amounts of types of chemicals to control acidity, alkalinity, firming, foaming, and moisture content, maturing, and anticaking. With gusto we eat our buffers, binders, bleachers, texturizers, and separators. Gramma is out of garlic, so she shakes a little allyl disulfide, to simulate garlic, in the salad dressing.

And here comes the best part—candies, each a different flavor. They're all artificial, though no one can tell but a chemist. We have black walnut (acetaldehyde), root-beer (made of methyl salicylate), peach (of anisic alcohol) and strawberry (with allyl caproate). The pineapple flavored candy is the most complex creation of all (except the coffee piece, which demanded a mixture of more than 300 compounds to make). The pineapple contains acetic acid, butyric acid, allyl caproate (again), isopentyl acetate, isopentyl isovalerate, caproic acid, ethyl crotonate, terpinyl proprioinate, ethyl butyrate, ethyl acetate, and several others, totaling seventeen chemicals.

Of course, we only had a miniscule amount of each chemical, which is what we told the undertaker when twenty years later my sister died of cancer, conceivably caused by chemicals accumulated in her bloodstream, where it fed the cells of her brain, lungs, liver, heart and all other parts. If you think this food is futuristic, let me tell you something hideous: *All of this was copied of off labels at my supermarket!*

Sales charts and financial ledgers weigh more heavily than the health of the nation.

Hyperkinetic Learning Disabilities and Food Synthetics

It's estimated that four to five million American children have a problem called hyperkinetic learning disability. This has been considered a form of minimal brain dysfunction; a neurological handicap. These children are neither mentally ill, nor mentally retarded, and their brains are not damaged.

Behaviorally, the problem shows itself as an impulse disorder. Symptoms range from mild to uncontrollable. Children are hyperactive, highly impulsive, and lack ability to control themselves. They engage in unpredictable bits of bizarre behavior. They exhibit excessive fidgetiness, jiggling, wiggling, distractability and unhappiness. They are cranky, crabby, surly, and compulsively disruptive. They have frequent temper tantrums and other outbursts of outrageous behavior, keeping everything in chaos. They endanger themselves, disregard others, and generate hazards and havoc wherever they go. Because they can't sit through a meal or a lesson, they do not learn in school, nor do they learn how to behave as expected at each age level.

Adherence to psychosocially sound childraising practices—not too restrictive, not too permissive, not too inconsistent, and rooted in love—makes a great difference, of course it always does, but there's much more to this problem than "family management."

Approximately 50 percent of the H-LD children are being given behavior management drugs. Amphetamines have been used for thirty years with this bewildering problem (Ritalin being the chief of these), because though amphetamines are *stimulants* to most people, they seem to calm down the hyperkinetic child. Side effects such as insomnia, lack of appetite, weight loss, nervousness, stomach ache and skin rash are common. Antianxiety drugs such as Librium, Miltown, Equanil, etc., are used too. They have more serious side effects.

Specialists have come up with all sorts of theories as to the causes of this condition, but Dr. Ben F. Feingold, a periatrician turned allergist, seems to have found the answer. He realized that the incidence of hyperkinetic learning disabilities has been rising since World War II, *exactly* as has been the practice of putting chemical food flavorings, colorings, and other additives into almost everything. Through carefully controlled study of children's diet, Dr. Feingold's initial hypothesis has hardened. He, and many other experts, are now convinced that in a particular group of children genetically so predisposed, synthetic food additives tamper with the brain and nervous system and short-circuit some of their functions.

All synthetics and natural salicylates must be entirely eliminated from the diet. First, parents are taught what to look for on labels, and what categories of food are out altogether. Then, parents monitor children's diets and train the children intensively for two or three weeks. Detailed diet records are kept. Management is gradually turned over to the child. Drug therapy, which may have lasted a lifetime, can be phased out! Fifty percent of these children improve markedly. Others, who have weak, wavery parents or who are too spoiled and stubborn, yield to temptation, fail to stick to the diet, and have to stay on drugs.

The current status of nutrition research in this country isn't much to write home about. Until recently, research has involved only single substances and has not concerned itself with how substances *combine*. Focus has been on nutritional *deficiencies,* not on poisons introduced into the body through diet. The fact is that agriculture schools know more about animal nutrition than medical schools and nutritional departments know about nutrition and the human being.

Immense health and mental health improvement may be as close as the kitchen cupboard for the hyperkinetic children—and for the rest of us as well.

CHAPTER NINETEEN:

Summary of How to Convert the Kids from What They Eat to What They Oughta and (The Hard Part) Starting to Do It

Our society and the citizens in it, spend huge sums on health cures (and on unsuccessful attempts at cure). We spend very little on health care. Participation in risk-reduction preventive health practices such as those suggested in this book is one way we can take a step in the direction of better health. Personal genetics count for a lot. Germs, viruses and accidents can be fatal. Everyone has individual biology.

Probably science should develop techniques to test each baby for individual biological needs so 21st Century pediatricians will be able to plan accurate personal diets. All evidence is that variations in need for this or that vitamin, amino acid, or mineral are enormous in many kinds of animals, so we can safely assume this to be the case with the animal homo sapien as well.

People who finish this conversion project may want to go futher—there's much further to go. But there are other books about that.

Still, no matter *how* far we go with developing health and attempting to prevent disaster, disease is part of life, and so is death, even for Adelle Davis.

In the meantime, if we supply the cells in our vital organs with inferior or merely "adequate" diets, diseases and disabilities of every description do develop. Feeding ourselves and our children wisely seems a better bet.

COMPARISON COLUMN:
Compare your typical daily diet to the following to see what *you* need to work on, and where you get a star to start with!

1. FRUIT
Three fruits or fruit juices daily, one a citrus if possible.
(Four if you *really* want it. Two if you prefer.)
(Canned fruit drink, powdered fruit flavored drinks, etc., are not juice.)

2. VEGETABLES
One green and one yellow vegetable daily.
(Plus as many more of any "unlimited" vegetables as you want.)
The body also needs *polyunsaturated vegetable oil* such as corn oil. Use in cooking, baking, salads and margarines.

3. MEAT
A serving of beef, veal, or lamb *no more than* three or four times a week, including breakfast meat, lunch meat, etc.
(Or meat as an *ingredient* no more than seven times a week.)
(It is not necessary to eat meat. If you don't eat meat, eat more fish, nuts, legumes, and dairy products.)

4. EGGS & CHEESE
No more than 3 eggs a week for breakfast, in egg salad, etc. (Skip eggs if you hate them. Eat more eggs if you love them and the doctor says OK.)
Cheese no more than one small serving a day, "straight" or as an ingredient. Eat as much cottage cheese as you want.

5. FISH & POULTRY
Fish and poultry at least twice a week each. (Or as often as you want.)

6. LEGUMES, CERTAIN NUTS, SEEDS
Legumes, nuts*, seeds**, as ingredients or snacks on meatless days, or as an extra once-a-day snack.
*Soy or peanuts only (unsalted are best)
**Sunflower, popcorn, sesame, etc.

7. WHOLE GRAIN
Three or four slices of whole grain bread daily, or the equivalent of other whole grain foods. Cereal*, brown rice, brown noodles, a dessert made with grain, etc.

*Do not buy sugar-coated cereal or baked products made with white flour.

8. DAIRY PRODUCTS
Two to four glasses of skim, 1% or 2% milk daily, or the equivalent (cottage cheese, yogurt, ice milk).*
* Regular ice cream doesn't count here, it's a treat; *not* a recommended daily dairy product. (Avoid butter. Use corn oil margarine.)

9. SUGAR AND SALT
The body gets all the sugar it needs for energy from natural foods.
Except for treats a few times a week, avoid sugar foods and situations that will tempt you to eat them:
—sugar
—soft drinks
—store
  —candy
  —pies
  —cakes
  —cookies
  —baked dessert snacks
  —syrups
  —jams and jellies
(Eat *homemade* foods like this; at least they can be made with *whole wheat* flour.)
Salt—Do not salt food. Avoid salted chips, pretzels, seeds, nuts and so on.

10. CHEMICALS
Read labels. Beware of chemicals. Don't buy brands containing artificial coloring, artificial flavoring, or preservatives such as BHA, BHT, nitrites, and nitrates.
Don't worry about once-in-a-while, but try hard to avoid the 3800 chemicals in today's foods!
Adults: Avoid more than a small amount of coffee, tea and alcohol.

A TEN MONTH CONVERSION FROM WHAT WE EAT TO WHAT WE "OUGHTA"

CONVERSION DIRECTIONS:

Test yourself. Eat exactly as you usually do. Write down every single thing you eat and drink and nibble. Don't forget anything! Do this for a week. Compare to the COMPARISON COLUMN (on right side of poster). Put a gold star on any of the ten segments you *already* are OK on. The others are the eating habits *you personally* need to work on if you aim to "eat healthier."

Each month, starting with 1st Month, concentrate *only* on the food category you choose. Pin the label of your choice in the top cube of the current month. *Don't take on too much at once.* When you finish a month successfully, put a gold star on it.

After the 1st Month, while focusing on the new food area, *be sure to keep up what you accomplished during the month(s) before.* Keep up the good work, and give the cube (yourself!) a gold star *for each month* that you stay converted.

BASIC IDEA:

1. **EAT MORE:**
   —fruits and fruit juices
   —vegetables and vegetable juices
   —fish and poultry
   —skim milk dairy products
   —legumes, nuts, seeds
   —whole grain foods

   WHY?
   More vitamins, minerals, proteins with less calories, cholesterol, chemicals, sugar and salt.

2. **EAT LESS:**
   —MEAT (avoid all "pig" meat— bacon, ham, sausage, pork, hot dogs)
   —eggs, cheese
   —chemicals, sugar, salt

   WHY?
   Less calories, cholesterol possibly heart attack and cancer producing chemicals, sugar and salt

3. **EAT ONLY AT PARTIES AND, *UNUSUAL* SPECIAL EVENTS (ONCE OR TWICE A MONTH?):**
   —junk food and excessively sugary, salted or rich foods.

   WHY?
   Exceptions and fun are important, too. Who wants to be good all the time?

IF AT FIRST YOU DON'T SUCCEED, TRY, TRY, AGAIN.

Converters start here

| 1st Month | 2nd Month | 3rd Month | 4th Month | 5th Month |

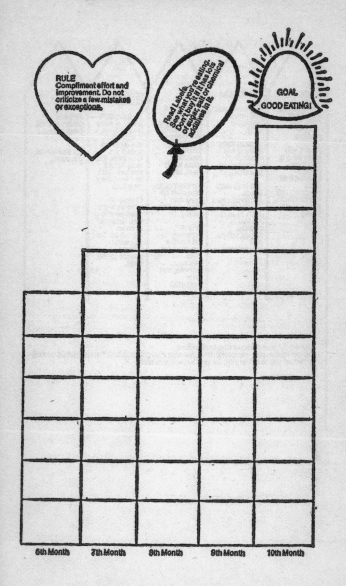

FRUIT

Three fruits or
fruit juices
daily, one
citrus if
possible.

(Four if you
really want it.
Two if you
prefer.)
(Canned fruit
drink,
powdered fruit
flavored drinks,
etc., are *not*
juice.)

VEGETABLES

One green and
one yellow
vegetable
daily.

(Plus as many
more of any
"unlimited"
vegetables as
you want.)

The body also
needs
polyunsaturated
vegetable oil
such as corn
oil. Use in
cooking,
baking, salads
and
margarines.

MEAT

A serving of
beef, veal, or
lamb *no more
than* three or
four times a
week,
including
breakfast,
meat, lunch
meat, etc.

(Or meat as an
ingredient no
more than
seven times a
week.)

(It is not
necessary to
eat meat. If
you don't eat
meat, eat more
fish, nuts,
legumes, and
dairy
products.)

**EGGS &
CHEESE**

No more than
3 eggs a week
for breakfast,
in egg salad,
etc. (Skip the
eggs if you
hate them. Eat
more eggs if
you love them
and the doctor
says OK.)

Cheese no
more than one
small serving a
day, "straight"
or as an
ingredient. Eat
as much
cottage
cheese as you
want.

**FISH &
POULTRY**

Fish and
poultry at least
twice a week
each.

(Or as often as
you want.)

Markers for Your Personal Conversion Chart
Cut out each marker separately. Glue on heavy paper. Thumb tack the appropriate marker
to "where you're at" on your bar graph conversion chart.

LEGUMES, CERTAIN NUTS, SEEDS

Legumes, nuts,* seeds,** as ingredients or snacks on meatless days, or as an extra once-a-day snack.

*Soy or peanuts only (unsalted are best)

**Sunflower, popcorn, sesame, etc.

WHOLE GRAIN

Three or four slices of whole grain bread daily, or the equivalent of other whole grain foods.

Cereal*, brown rice, brown noodles, a dessert made with grain, etc.

*Do not buy sugar-coated cereal or baked products made with white flour.

DAIRY PRODUCTS

Two to four glasses of skim, 1% or 2% milk daily, or the equivalent (cottage cheese, yogurt, ice milk.*).

(Avoid butter, use corn oil margarine.)

*Regular ice cream doesn't count here, it's a treat, *not* a recommended daily dairy product.

SUGAR & SALT

The body gets all the sugar it needs for energy from natural foods.

Except for treats a few times a week, avoid sugar foods and situations that will tempt you to eat them:
—sugar
—soft drinks
—store
——candy*
——pies
——cakes
——cookies
——baked dessert snacks
——syrups
——jams & jellies
*Eat *homemade* foods like this; at least they can be made with whole wheat flour.

Salt
Do not salt food.
Avoid salted chips, pretzels, seeds, nuts and so on.

CHEMICALS

Read labels. Beware of chemicals. Don't buy brands containing artificial coloring, artificial flavoring or preservatives such as BHA, BHT, nitrates and nitrates.

Don't worry about once-a-in-a-while, but try hard to avoid the 3800 chemicals in today's foods!

Recommended Reading

Cooking Without Meat. Marshall Cavendish Publications, Lmtd., London, 1973.
   Over 300 fantastic dishes with color photos.
Creative Food Experiences for Children. Mary T. Goodwin & Gerry Pollen. Center for Science in the Public Interest, Washington, D. C., 1974.
   A curriculum in book form, full of food projects. Perfect for teachers of young children. Great for parents, too!
Earth Water Fire Air. Barbara Friedlander. Collier Books, New York, 1972.
   The food photographs inspire pure eating.
Fabulous Fiber Cookbook. Jeanne Jones. 101 Productions, San Francisco, 1977.
Food and Fitness. Blue Cross Association, 840 N. Lake Shore Drive, Chicago, Illinois 60611, 1973.
   A collection of pieces by experts on why to exercise and eat right.
Forever Thin. Theodore Isaac Rubin, M.D., Bernard Geis Associates, 1970.
   By a psychoanalyst obesity expert. Explains why some people become and stay obese.
Growing Up Thin. Alvin N. Eden, M.D. with Joan Rattner Hellman. David McKay Co., Inc., New York, 1975.
   A pediatrician tells how and why to fatproof your child.
Health Foods, Facts and Fakes. Sidney Margolius, Walker & Co., New York, 1973.
   An evaluation of the controversies raging within and around the health food movement.
Let's Cook It Right. Adelle Davis, New American Library, 1970, New York.

A vast amount of information as well as recipes galore.

Nutrition Against Disease, Environmental Protection. Roger J. Williams. Pitman Publishing Corp., New York, 1971.

Nutrition Scoreboard, A Guide to Better Eating. Center for Science in the Public Interest, Washington, D. C., Michael Jacobson, 1973.

Today's peculiar foods and how they compare to some of the old fashioned foods. Motivational.

Recipes for a Small Planet. Ellen Buchman Ewald. Ballantine Books, New York, 1973.

The delicious solution to the high cost of meat—high protein meatless cooking.

Reduce and Stay Reduced. Norman Jolliffe, M.D., Simon and Schuster, New York, 1963.

The Natural Foods Cookbook. Beatrice Trum Hunter, Simon & Schuster, New York, 1961.

You can learn a lot while you eat super well.

The Supermarket Handbook: Access to Whole Foods. Nikki and David Goldbeck, Harper & Row, New York, 1974.

This should help on the front line.

Why Your Child Is Hyperactive. Ben F. Feingold, M.D., Random House, New York, 1975.

How food additives affect some children's behavior.